MARYLAND'S FLAVOR

To Dolf and family
Christmas 1981
So you'll remember us!

From the Allegheny Mountains
to the sands
of the Eastern Shore

D1609637

American Cancer Society, Maryland Division, Inc.

There is no such thing as a book of entirely new and original recipes and no originality is claimed for the recipes contained in this book. This book represents a collection of favorite recipes submitted by contributors who vouch for their excellence.

International Standard Book Number -0-939114-03-8

First printing June, 1981 35,000 books

Printed in the United States of America

WIMMER BROTHERS FINE PRINTING & LITHOGRAPHY
Memphis, Tennessee 38118
*"Cookbooks of Distinction"*tm

James A. Michener, a resident of St. Michaels, Maryland, and famous author of *Chesapeake* and *The Covenant* has shared with us his impressions of Eastern Shore cooking.

Each summer and autumn travelers come from hundreds of miles around to revel in the delights of the Eastern Shore: crabs in summer, oysters in autumn. I know of few regions in the United States with such a distinctive cuisine, and such a delightful one. But equally good are the excellent fruits, melons and vegetables from our farms. This cannot be called a gourmet's paradise, because the cooking is plain and strong and simple. But it is an American marvel.

Most sincerely,

James A. Michener

James A. Michener
Honorary Cookbook Chairman

FORWARD

It has been with a great deal of pleasure and pride that I have served as State Chairman for Maryland's Flavor. The hours that I've spent have given me a chance to share something very special—the enthusiasm and spirit of the volunteers across the state.

Special thanks to John Moll for our cover. James Michener for serving as honorary chairman and Pat Ryan. Dorothy Kraybill, Martha Gebo, Elois Reynolds, Phyllis Mason, Barbara Benussi, Angie Linn and Nancy Dick for helping to assemble our book.

I wish that we could have used every delicious recipe and all the artwork submitted. We hope that you will delight in trying the recipes that have been included.

It is evident that Maryland volunteers have joined the two million volunteers all over the nation that are searching for "the greatest recipe of all—the cure for cancer."

Fondly,

Ginger Brinsfield

Ginger Brinsfield

Indicates Volunteer Cookbook Chairman for Unit.

Contributing Artist:

John Moll
Alice Frederick
P.K. Trump
Gerry Spore
Lynne Davis
Pat Merchant
Alan H. Archambault
Andrew Yff
David Michael
Mary Moore
Harriet Reichard
Barbara Roman
Selman Wright
Tara Moore

Paul Lockhart
Marcy Shear Wolpe
Ruth Westfall
Jane Trout
Gaines Reynolds Clore
David A. Dulik
Ronald Hall
M.B. Gordan
Beebe Winterbottom
Don Kimball
Chuck Harness
David Moorehead
Claire LeCompte

TABLE OF CONTENTS

RECIPE FOR PRESERVING CHILDREN

1 large grassy field
6 small children, all sizes
3 dogs
Narrow strip of brook

Pebbles, if possible
A deep blue sky
Hot sun
Flowers

Mix the children with dogs, empty into field, stirring continuously. Sprinkle the field with flowers, pour brook gently over the pebbles. Cover all with deep blue sky and bake in hot sun. When children are well browned, they may be removed. Will be found right and ready for setting away to cool in the bath tub.

Garrett County Unit

RECIPE FOR HAPPINESS

2 heaping cups patience
1 heartful love
2 handsful generosity

Dash of laughter
1 headful of
    understanding

Sprinkle generously with kindness and add plenty of faith; mix well. Spread over a period of a lifetime and serve to everyone you meet.

Calvert County Unit

Appetizers

Mt. Lake Park Hotel—Sketch by Alice Frederick

The central portion of this Garrett County hotel was built in 1882. During the next 15 years its guest facilities were doubled. The hotel was the center of many important social functions and for 60 years after its enlargement provided fine accommodations and delectable cuisine for its guests.

GEFELTE FISH

15 pounds combination
  rock, whitefish and
  pike
4 eggs
6 large onions,
  quartered

4 carrots, quartered
1 tablespoon salt
1 teaspoon white
  pepper
$3/4$ teaspoon sugar

Have fish market clean, bone, and skin fish, reserving bones and skin to take home. This should leave about $7\frac{1}{2}$ pounds fish meat which should then be ground. Add one egg at a time to ground fish, beating after each addition. Add salt, pepper and sugar. Meanwhile, in a large pot, place fish skin, heads and bones; cover with water. Add carrots and onions and seasonings. Simmer about 45 minutes. Strain, taste and adjust seasonings. Return broth to pot. Shape fish mixture into egg-shaped balls and drop into boiling broth. Simmer slowly for about 30 minutes, shaking pot so fish balls won't stick.
Note: Can be eaten hot but they're better chilled and served on lettuce leaves with horseradish. Makes 40.

Sonia Lowitz
Northwest Community Unit (Baltimore)

ZUCCHINI PIZZA

Large zucchini (number
  of servings depends on
  size and number of
  zucchini)
Salt
1 tablespoon pizza
  sauce
1 teaspoon chopped
  black olives

1 teaspoon minced
  green onion
2 tablespoons
  shredded
  mozzarella,
  Monterey Jack
  or other white
  cheese

Preheat broiler, placing rack about 5 inches from heat source. Cut zucchini into slices $1/4$-inch thick; salt lightly. On each slice, place sauce, olives, green onion and cheese. Place on baking sheet and broil until cheese is melted and bubbly, about 4 to 5 minutes (zucchini should be crisp). Serve warm.

Hon. Gladys Noon Spellman
Greater Laurel Beltsville Unit (Laurel)

CHEESE BALLS

1 (6-ounce) package
cream cheese
1 jar Kraft Old English
cheese
1 jar Kraft Roka Blue
cheese

1 tablespoon
Worcestershire sauce
1 tablespoon mashed
onion
Chopped nuts
Chopped parsley

Leave the above items at room temperature for about 3 hours. Mix all ingredients (except nuts and parsley) together and place in refrigerator to harden, about 1 hour. Roll into 2 large balls and then over nuts and parsley, which have been spread on a large piece of waxed paper. Wrap in clean waxed paper and chill or freeze. Yield: 2 balls.

Louisa Noble
Montgomery County Unit (Silver Spring)

Variations: Add ¼ cup maraschino cherries, drained and 1 tablespoon maraschino cherry juice (optional-for color only). Or add 1 cup crushed pineapple, drained, and up to 3 tablespoons wine vinegar.

Sandra W. Younger
Calvert County Unit (St. Leonard)

Emma Knapp
South Anne Arundel County Unit (Shady Side)

Louise Messenger
Garrett County Unit (Oakland)

TUNA DIP

1 (7-ounce) can tuna
3 ounces cream cheese
¼ teaspoon garlic salt
¼ teaspoon celery salt
¼ teaspoon onion salt

¼ teaspoon Accent
3 to 6 tablespoons
mayonnaise
½ teaspoon soy sauce
1 teaspoon horseradish

Mix early in the day. Refrigerate. Serve with corn chips.

Charlene Filewicz
Caroline County Unit (Denton)

CRABMEAT DIP

1 can cream of mushroom
  soup
1 tablespoon unflavored
  gelatin (softened in 3
  tablespoons water)
6 ounces cream cheese

2 green onions, finely
  chopped
8 ounces fresh crabmeat
1 cup finely chopped
  celery
1 cup mayonnaise

In a saucepan heat undiluted cream of mushroom soup until hot.
Remove from heat and add gelatin and water mixture. Allow to
cool slightly. Mix softened cream cheese and mayonnaise well
and add to saucepan. Combine the remaining ingredients and
pour into greased mold. Set in refrigerator overnight. Unmold on
plate and serve with assorted crackers.

Barbara Moll
Southern Charles County Unit (LaPlata)
Similar recipes submitted by:
Sharon Robertson
Queen Annes County Unit
Judy Pinder
Cecil County Unit (Elkton)
Carolyn B. Lister
Carroll County Unit (Westminster)
Irma Z. Myers
Annapolis Unit (Annapolis)
Doris W. Tettimer
Calvert County Unit

HERB CURRY DIP

1 cup salad dressing
1/2 cup sour cream
1 teaspoon crushed
  mixed herbs
1/4 teaspoon salt
1/8 teaspoon curry powder
1 tablespoon snipped
  parsley

1 tablespoon grated
  onion
1 1/2 teaspoons lemon juice
1/2 teaspoon
  Worcestershire sauce

Blend all ingredients. Chill well. Serve with carrot and celery
sticks, cauliflower buds and radishes.

Louise Messenger
Garrett County

CHILI CON QUESO DIP

1 pound ground beef
1 medium onion, chopped
1 teaspoon lemon pepper
1½ tablespoons garlic salt
1 small can chopped
  green chili pepper
1 (8-ounce) can tomato
  sauce

1 can cream of
  mushroom soup
1½ pounds American
  cheese
Hot sauce (Red Hot,
  Tabasco, etc) to taste

Sauté ground beef, chopped onion, lemon pepper, garlic salt; pour off grease. Add tomato sauce, chopped green chili pepper and cream of mushroom soup, stirring frequently. When piping hot or bubbly, add cheese slowly, stirring continuously; add hot sauce to desired flavor. Serve hot with corn chips or fresh vegetables. Yield: 1½ quarts
Note: This recipe takes 25 minutes preparation time and can be made in an electric skillet using medium heat.

Carol Lynn Nichols
Greater Laurel-Beltsville Unit (Laurel)

PEPPERED CHEDDAR DIP

1½ cups dairy sour
  cream
1 cup shredded Cheddar
  cheese
¼ cup finely chopped
  onion

3 tablespoons minced
  green pepper
¼ teaspoon red pepper
  sauce (Tabasco)
1 tablespoon milk

Mix together all ingredients in a medium-sized mixing bowl, stirring with a spoon. Cover; refrigerate at least 1 hour before serving. Serve with crisp slices of celery and carrots. Yield: 2 cups
Note: If necessary add another tablespoon of milk to make a good dipping consistency.

Deborah Rhoades
Severna Park Unit (Severna Park)

SAUSAGE BALLS

½ pound mild pork
sausage
½ pound hot pork sausage

½ to 1 pound sharp
Cheddar cheese,
3 to 4 cups Bisquick

Preheat oven to 350⁰ degrees. In a medium sized bowl, mix the sausage, cheese and Bisquick until well blended. Form the mixture into small balls (about the size of a small gum ball). Place the balls on a slightly greased cookie sheet. Bake for 10 to 15 minutes turning them over once halfway through the cooking time. Remove when golden brown. Serve with toothpicks. Yield: about 45 sausage balls.
Note: Can be made ahead and frozen. Good to have in the freezer when company drops in.

Susanne Schwarz
East Baltimore County Unit (Baltimore)

Ruth Fulcher
South Potomac Unit (Temple Hill)

ARTICHOKE QUICHE

1 bunch spring onions,
chopped
1 tablespoon butter
2 (6-ounce) jars
marinated artichoke
hearts
6 drops Tabasco sauce

6 ounces sharp Cheddar
cheese, grated
6 saltine squares,
crushed
Salt and pepper
4 eggs

Sauté onions in butter. Drain artichokes and cut up fine. Mix artichokes, onions, Tabasco, grated cheese, crushed saltines, salt, and pepper. Place mixture in quiche dish or greased 9-inch pie pan. Beat eggs well and pour over artichoke mixture. Bake at 350 degrees for 35 minutes.

Beryl Sachs
Northwest Community Unit (Baltimore)

MARINATED VEGETABLE HORS D'OEUVRES

1 small cauliflower
(broken into flowerets)
2 green peppers, cut into
1/2-inch strips
1/2 pound small mushroom
caps
1 (5 1/4-ounce) can pitted
black olives, drained
1 (4 1/2-ounce) jar white
cocktail onions, drained

3/4 cup olive oil
1/4 cup salad oil
1/4 cup Minute Maid
100% pure lemon juice
1 1/4 cups white vinegar
1/4 cup sugar
2 teaspoons salt
1 teaspoon ground pepper
1 clove garlic, minced

Mix vegetables together in a shallow dish. Bring remaining ingredients to a boil; cook 5 minutes and pour over vegetables. Cover and marinate for 24 hours in the refrigerator. Drain and serve with toothpicks or as an appetizer/antipasto.

Angie McCusker
Frederick County Unit (Frederick)

TAMALE MEATBALLS

1 1/2 pounds lean ground
beef
2 cups crumbled corn
bread
1/2 teaspoon salt
1 (10-ounce) can
enchilada sauce,
divided

1 (8-ounce) can tomato
sauce
1/2 cup grated Monterey
Jack cheese

Combine meat, corn bread, salt and 1/2 cup enchilada sauce. Mix well. Shape into 1-inch sized balls. Place in a 15-x-10-x-1-inch jelly roll pan and bake at 350 degrees for 20 to 30 minutes. Drain on paper towels. Combine remaining enchilada sauce and tomato sauce, heating slowly until well blended. To serve, place meatballs in chafing dish, pour sauce over and top with cheese.

Mrs. J.M. West
Annapolis Unit (Annapolis)

GUESS WHAT IT IS APPETIZER

1 (8½-ounce) can
artichoke hearts in
water
1 cup mild Cheddar
cheese, shredded

1 cup mayonnaise
1 (10¾-ounce) can
cream of mushroom
soup

Drain and cut artichoke hearts into small pieces. Combine all ingredients; mix well. Pour into an oven-proof serving dish. Heat for 30 minutes or until very bubbly in a 350 degree oven. Serve hot with crackers or small toast points.
Note: I sometimes serve it with mini pastry cups purchased in a cheese shop, placing them on a small tray next to the hot dish where guests can spoon it into them at the buffet table.

Mrs. Evelyn Martone
Kent County Unit (Chestertown)

CHEESE HOOIES

½ pound butter or
margarine
½ pound shredded sharp
Cheddar cheese
2 cups sifted flour

1 teaspoon salt
Dash of cayenne pepper

Cream shredded cheese with softened butter. Add salt and cayenne. Work in flour with fork or slotted spoon. Knead on lightly floured board until smooth. Roll into a long thin roll. Refrigerate for 2 hours or more. Slice thinly and place on lightly greased cookie sheet about ½-inch apart. Bake at 350 degrees for 8 to 10 minutes. Remove pan from oven and place cheese rounds on a cake rack to cool.

Betty Walters
Annapolis Unit (Annapolis)
Variation submitted by
Georgia M. Hensel
Worcester County Unit (Snow Hill)

CRABBIE

½ cup butter or
  margarine, softened
1 (6-ounce) jar Old
  English cheese spread
½ teaspoon garlic salt

½ teaspoon seasoned salt
1 ½ tablespoons
  mayonnaise
1 (7-ounce) can crabmeat
6 English muffins

Let butter and cheese soften. Blend with rest of ingredients. Spread on split English muffins. Freeze for at least 30 minutes. Remove from freezer 5 minutes before using. Cut each round into 6 pie-shaped pieces. Broil until they puff up and are bubbly and slightly golden brown. Serve hot. Yield: 48 or more hot hors d'oeuvres.

Sis LeGates
Talbot County Unit (Easton)
Lois Nagle
Bel Air Unit (Bel Air)

CHEESE PUFFS

2 cups shredded sharp
  Cheddar cheese
½ cup soft butter
1 cup sifted flour

½ teaspoon salt
1 teaspoon paprika
48 (or more) small stuffed
  olives

Blend cheese with butter. Add sifted dry ingredients. Mold a teaspoon of mixture around each olive covering completely. Bake at 400 degrees for 15 minutes.
Note: May be baked and then frozen on a cookie sheet. When needed, remove from freezer one hour before using. Heat in a hot oven for a few minutes. Easy, good, and always ready in the freezer.

Mrs. Marjorie Golze
Montgomery County Unit (Bethesda)

BACON BREADSTICKS

1 package thin
breadsticks
1/2 slice bacon for each
breadstick, cut
lengthwise

1/2 cup grated Parmesan
cheese

Dip bacon in Parmesan cheese; wrap bacon around breadstick. Roll breadstick in more cheese. Bake on drip rack at 400 degrees until bacon browns.
Note: For microwave-microwave 6 to 7 minutes on full power on drip rack.

Mrs. Dusti Jones
Kent County Unit (Chestertown)

AMIEE'S MOCK ESCARGOTS

1 pound fresh
mushrooms, cleaned
1/2 cup butter

6 large cloves of garlic
1 tablespoon parsley

Cut mushroom stems even with mushroom; do *not* pull out the entire stem. Melt butter in large pan. Put garlic through a press or grate it so that it is in small pieces; add garlic to butter; sauté but do *not* allow to brown. Add parsley. Lower heat to simmer and add mushrooms, stirring constantly for about 4 minutes.
Note: *Can be served as an appetizer or side dish.*

Amy LaParle
Alleghany County Unit (Cumberland)

CHILES QUICKI

3 small cans green chiles
1 bar Crackerbarrel
sharp cheese

3 eggs
3 tablespoons milk

Chop chiles and line a 9-inch pie plate with them. Spread shredded cheese over chiles. Mix eggs with milk and pour over cheese. Bake at 325 degrees for 25 minutes.
Note: *Can be prepared early and reheated when served.*

Doris Levine
Montgomery County Unit (Silver Spring)

STUFFED MUSHROOMS PARMIGIANA

12 large fresh
  mushrooms
2 tablespoons butter or
  margarine
1 medium onion, finely
  chopped
2 ounces pepperoni,
  diced
1/4 cup finely chopped
  green pepper
1 small garlic clove,
  minced

1/2 cup finely crushed Ritz
  crackers (12 crackers)
3 tablespoons grated
  Parmesan cheese
1 tablespoon snipped
  parsley
1/2 teaspoon oregano
1/2 teaspoon seasoned salt
Dash pepper
1/3 cup chicken broth

Wash the mushrooms and remove stems. Finely chop stems and reserve. Drain caps on paper towels. Melt butter or margarine in skillet; add onion, pepperoni, green pepper, garlic, and chopped mushroom stems. Cook until vegetables are tender but not brown. Add cracker crumbs, cheese, parsley, seasoned salt, oregano, and pepper; mix well. Stir in chicken broth. Spoon stuffing into mushroom caps, rounding tops. Place caps in shallow baking pan with about 1/4-inch of water covering bottom of pan. Bake, uncovered, in a 325-degree oven about 25 minutes or until heated through. Yield: 12 stuffed mushrooms.

Judith M. Megee
Aberdeen/Havre de Grace Unit (Rising Sun)

TUNA PATÉ

2 (6 1/2-ounce) cans tuna,
  drained
1 (8-ounce) package of
  cream cheese
1 teaspoon instant onion

2 tablespoons parsley
2 tablespoons chili sauce
1/2 teaspoon hot pepper
  sauce (bottled)

Mix all ingredients together at once, blending well. Pat into a small mold (2 cup size). Chill for at least 3 hours. Turn over on a dish and surround it with crackers of your choice. Spread on crackers to serve.

Elaine Skowronski
Frederick County Unit (Frederick)

APPETIZERS

POOR MAN'S LIVER PATÉ (WITH CAVIAR)

1 pound liverwurst
Garlic powder
Basil
Worcestershire sauce
1 tablespoon minced
  fresh onions
2 ounces cream cheese

Tabasco sauce
Mayonnaise
2 ounces black or red
  caviar (lump fish)
Slice of lemon or sprig
  of holly
Wheat or rye crackers

Soften liverwurst, add garlic powder, basil and Worcestershire sauce to taste. Add minced onions. Refrigerate 24 hours. Soften cream cheese. Add garlic powder, Tabasco sauce and mayonnaise to spreading consistency. (Be cautious with Tabasco unless you like things very spicy.) Form liverwurst mixture into a ball. Cover top and sides with cream cheese mixture. Spread caviar over the top. Decorate with lemon slice or holly sprig. Serve with crackers.
Note: Delicious! Guaranteed to receive comments of praise. A favorite with adults. Easy and quick.

Frances Ann Gilbert
Frederick County Unit (Frederick)

SPICY BITES

1 pound hot sausage
1 pound ground beef

1 pound Velveeta cheese
Party rye bread

In a 10-inch skillet brown the sausage. Remove from pan leaving the grease. Brown the ground beef in the sausage grease and then drain. Return the sausage to the pan with the ground beef. Coarsely chop the Velveeta and add to the meat mixture. Mix the cheese and meat together over low heat until the cheese is melted. Spread the mixture on party rye bread. Bake in a 450-degree oven for approximately 6 minutes or until slightly browned. Yield: about 60 appetizers.
Note: This mixture freezes well and is also tasty spread on English muffins and broiled.

Mrs. Lucy G. Fielding
Mid Anne Arundel Unit (Millersville)

Beverages

Mt. Airey—Sketch by P.K. Trump

In 1830 there was only a settlement of houses and stores along Parr's Ridge. History says Irish B. & O. Railroad workmen whose ears were freezing named this Carroll County area Mt. Airey. Today Mt. Airey is the home for many who work along the Baltimore Washington industrial corridor as well as families who have lived there for generations.

GLOGG (SWEDISH CHRISTMAS BREW)

1 cup water
1 cup sugar
6 whole cloves
12 cardamon seeds
1 orange peel
1 bottle Burgundy wine

1 cup Muscatel wine
1 cup vodka
1/2 cup blanched almonds
1/2 cup raisins
16 lumps of sugar

Mix together water, sugar and spices; simmer 1/2 hour; strain the spices. Add wines and vodka and heat to just below boiling. Put a few almonds, raisins and 1 lump of sugar in 16 mugs. Fill mugs with beverage and serve immediately. Yield: 16 servings.

Helena (Sis) Cheyne
Howard County Unit (Ellicott City)

MANLY'S IRISH CREAM LIQUEUR

3 eggs
1/2 pint cream
1 can sweetened
   condensed milk
1 1/3 teacups whiskey

1/3 teaspoon almond
   flavoring
1/4 teaspoon instant coffee
1 1/2 teaspoons chocolate
   (thick) topping

Whisk all ingredients together and refrigerate.

Arthur Manly
Aberdeen/Havre de Grace Unit (Havre de Grace)

BEVERAGE SPECIAL

Ginger ale or ginger
   beer
Coffee-flavored ice
   cream

Skim milk

For 1 glass:
Pour into tall glass in the following order: 1/2 bottle ginger ale or ginger beer, 2 tablespoons ice cream and enough skim milk to fill the glass. Stir gently and serve.
For the punchbowl:
Stir together 6 bottles of ginger beer, 1 quart ice cream and 1 quart skim milk. Fill individual servings.
Note: The thickness is nog (not a shake).

Serena G. Mills
Park Heights/Forest Park Unit (Baltimore)

FROTHY FRUIT PUNCH

1 (46-ounce) can
  pineapple juice, chilled
1 (46-ounce) can orange
  juice, chilled

2 pints sherbet, softened
6 (7-ounce) bottles 7-Up,
  chilled

Combine juices in punch bowl; add sherbet, stirring until partially blended. Pour 7-Up in slowly; stir gently to blend. Yield: 40 servings.

Bonnie Pittman
Allegany County Unit (LaVale)

MOCK PINK CHAMPAGNE

Freeze 1 bottle 7-Up with cranberries and well-washed holly leaves in a bell or heart-shaped salad mold the day before serving.

2 quarts cranberry juice
  cocktail

2 quarts lemon-lime
  carbonated beverage

Chill cranberry juice and beverages thoroughly. Pour equal quantities in punch bowl just before serving. Float 7-Up mold on top.
Note: May substitute diet cranberry juice and Sprite. Decorate around punch bowl with holly leaves and cranberries.

Jane Wobbeking
Southwest Baltimore Unit (Baltimore)

SLUSH PUNCH

4 cups sugar
6 cups water
2 (12-ounce) cans frozen
  orange juice
2 (12-ounce) cans frozen
  lemonade

1 (46-ounce) can
  pineapple juice
5 mashed bananas and/or
  2 (16-ounce) cans
  pineapple chunks
3 quarts gingerale

Bring water and sugar to a rapid boil, making a simple syrup. Add remaining ingredients except gingerale, and mix thoroughly. Freeze mixture. When ready to use, stir in gingerale. Yield: 5 quarts of slush mix.

Zilpha A. Pinkney
Marlboro/Aquasco Unit (Clinton)

AUNT MAY'S GRAPE WINE

1 quart Concord grapes,
   very ripe
2¹/₂ pounds granulated
   sugar

1 package dry yeast
¹/₂ cup raisins
Water

Wash grapes. Combine above ingredients in a gallon glass jar. Fill jar to top with tap water. Cover with several thicknesses of cheesecloth and tie around jar top. Set to ferment in a cool, dark place, approximately 6 weeks. Strain wine through muslin cloth. Discard grapes. Wash glass jar and return wine to glass jar. Do not close lid tightly. When ready to serve, strain again into wine containers.

Mrs. Ann S. Newsome
Kent County Unit (Worton)

KIR

8 ounces chilled dry
   Chablis or dry white
   wine
1 ounce chilled creme de
   casis

Ice cubes
Twist of lemon per
   glass

Mix wine and liqueur; pour over ice cubes; add twist of lemon. Serve in 6-ounce wine glass.

Nancy Urquhart Griffin Warren
Greater Laurel/Beltsville Unit (Laurel)

BABYCHAM SUNRISE

4 fifths (750 milliliter
   bottle) babycham
3 cups vodka
1 quart orange juice

1 pint orange sherbet
Sparkling mineral
   water

In a large punch bowl, combine babycham and vodka. Let chill for 1 hour. 30 minutes before serving, add sherbet and let stand at room temperature. Just before serving, add mineral water to sparkle.

Showerings Ltd.
Aberdeen/Havre de Grace Unit (Havre de Grace)

APPLE TODDY

6 apples, roasted
1/2 gallon water
1/2 gallon good whiskey
1 3/4 pounds granulated
    sugar
1/2 tablespoon allspice

1/2 tablespoon mace
1 lemon, sliced thin
1 orange, sliced thin
1 2-gallon non-metallic
    container, preferably
    an earthen crock

Place roasted apples in container. Boil water and pour over apples; add other ingredients. Let stand for several weeks, stirring occasionally. Strain into bottles.
Note: Serve in wine glasses, warning takers to sip gingerly! This is an old family recipe that my mother used to make at Christmas to add to the festive spirit when visitors called. It is calculated to stimulate fond memories!

James C. Mitchell
Southern Charles County Unit (LaPlata)

EGG NOG

1/3 cup sugar
2 eggs, separated
1/4 teaspoon salt
4 cups milk
3 tablespoons sugar
1 teaspoon vanilla

Brandy or rum
    (Flavoring may be
    substituted if desired)
1 cup whipping cream
Ground nutmeg

Beat the 1/3 cup sugar into egg yolks. Add salt; stir into milk. Cook and stir over medium heat until mixture coats a metal spoon; cool. Beat egg whites until foamy. Gradually add the 3 tablespoons sugar, beating to soft peaks. Add to egg yolk mixture and mix well. Add vanilla, liquor or flavoring to taste. Chill. Whip cream to soft peaks. Pour egg mixture into punch bowl; top with whipped cream and sprinkle with nutmeg. Yield: Eight 4-ounce servings.

Mary Jane Frere
Southern Charles County Unit (Bel Alton)

PUNCH FOR THIRTY

5 bananas
2 lemons
6 cups water
2 cups sugar
46 ounces pineapple
  juice

12 ounces concentrated
  orange juice
2 quarts ginger ale

Mash bananas through Foley food mill. Juice lemons and mix juice with bananas immediately. Boil water and sugar and cool mixture. Combine banana mixture, water mixture, pineapple juice, and orange juice. Freeze concoction. Before serving, add ginger ale so punch will be crushed and icy without ice having to be added.

Della A. Whittaker
Merle-Duvall Unit (Adelphi)

PORT WINE

1 quart grape juice
3 pounds sugar
3 quarts warm water

1 box raisins
1 cake of yeast

Work 10 days then strain through double cheese cloth. Put in bottles and let set for 10 days. Drink and be merry!

Richard E. Perkins
Lower Park Heights Unit (Baltimore)

HOT SPICED CIDER

1 teaspoon whole cloves
1 stick cinnamon
1 teaspoon whole allspice
2 quarts apple cider

1/2 cup brown sugar
1/4 teaspoon salt
1 orange (optional)
Whole cloves (optional)

Tie 1 teaspoon whole cloves, cinnamon and allspice in a small cloth bag. Mix cider, sugar and salt in a large saucepan; add spice bag. Heat to boiling, reduce heat and cover. Simmer for 20 minutes. Remove spice bag to serve. Stud orange with whole cloves and place in cider, if desired.
Note: May be prepared in a crock pot. Mix all ingredients and cook for 4 hours on low.

Mary Lee Woutila
Southeastern Baltimore County Unit (Baltimore)

Breads and Pastries

St. Ignatius Church—Hickory, Maryland

This is the original church which was built in 1792. It began as a Jesuit mission church. Several additions were made including the massive tower in front of the church in 1865. Nestled in a grove of magnificent oaks, this church has become a Harford County landmark. It is believed to be the oldest Catholic church in continuous use throughout the Archdiocese of Baltimore.

EASTERN SHORE CORNPONE

2 cups cornmeal, sifted
1/2 cup flour, sifted
1 teaspoon salt
2/3 cup sugar

1 stick margarine
3 cups boiling water
1 1/2 cups milk
3 eggs, beaten

Grease a 9-x-5-x-3 inch loaf pan or 2 quart baking dish. Preheat oven to 350 degrees. In a large mixing bowl, mix cornmeal, flour, salt and sugar. Lay a stick of margarine on top of these ingredients. Pour over 3 cups boiling water. Stir until smooth. Add eggs and milk. Stir until smooth again. Pour into pan and bake for 1 hour at 350 degrees.

Note: Let this bread cool for 2 to 3 hours before removing from the pan for easier slicing. My family likes it sliced, then browned in a frying pan and served with eggs for breakfast. And we always have it with fish!

Mildred T. Villani
Worcester County Unit (Berlin)
Similar recipe submitted by: Joan F. Smith
Kent County Unit (Chestertown)

SOUTHERN SPOON BREAD

3 cups milk
1 1/2 cups cornmeal
3 eggs, well beaten
1 teaspoon salt

2 tablespoons melted butter
1 3/4 teaspoons baking powder

Bring milk and cornmeal to a boil, making a mush. Cool slightly. Add eggs, salt, butter and baking powder. Mix well. Pour into a greased casserole dish and bake in a 350 degree oven for 35 to 40 minutes or until knife inserted in center comes out clean.

Mrs. Phillip Waalkes
Montgomery County Unit (Rockville)

BEER BREAD

1 (12-ounce) can beer,
    room temperature
3¹/₂ cups self-rising flour

¹/₄ cup sugar
2 eggs

Preheat oven to 375 degrees. Place beer (still sealed) in a bowl of hot water in an upright position. In a mixing bowl, place flour, sugar and eggs; add beer all at once; stir just enough to mix well. Pour batter into a greased 9-x-5-x-3 inch loaf pan and bake for about 1 hour. Yield: 1 loaf.
Note: After 40 minutes place aluminum foil over the top of the bread to avoid burning.

Kathy P. Discher
Cecil County Unit (Elkton)

NUT BREAD/FRUIT BREAD

4 cups flour
4 teaspoons baking
    powder
1 teaspoon salt
1 cup sugar
1 cup ground English
    walnuts and/or

1 cup candied fruit,
    chopped
3 eggs, lightly beaten
1¹/₂ cups milk

Preheat oven to 275 degrees. Sift flour, baking powder, sugar and salt together in a large bowl. Add ground walnuts and/or candied fruit, stirring until thoroughly mixed. Add eggs; mix thoroughly. Stir in milk, in small amounts, until a sticky dough is formed. Place dough in two greased 9-x-5-x-3 inch loaf pans. Let rise in a warm place for 20 minutes. Bake in a 275 degree oven for 45 to 60 minutes till a toothpick comes out dry when tested. Remove from pans and cool. When completely cool, wrap in wax paper and store in refrigerator. The bread is better the day after baking, and will keep stored for a week.
Note: This recipe was originally made with hickory nuts, not too readily available these days, and a nuisance to pick out! It was used by my grandmother, mother, and I have used it for 50 years or so. It is elegant for tea sandwiches with cream cheese or real butter!

Mrs. Thomas H. Hoffman
Talbot County Unit (Oxford)

CRANBERRY BREAD

2 cups sifted flour
1 1/2 teaspoons baking
powder
1/2 teaspoon baking soda
1/2 teaspoon salt
1 egg, well beaten
2 tablespoons shortening,
melted

3/4 cup sugar
3/4 cup orange juice, room
temperature
1/2 cup cranberries,
chopped
1/2 cup nuts, chopped

Sift together flour, baking powder, baking soda and salt three times; set aside. Mix sugar, egg and melted shortening; add orange juice and stir. Add this mixture to dry ingredients and mix until thoroughly moistened. Reserve a few cranberries and nuts to decorate top of loaf. Stir remaining cranberries and nuts into batter and pour into a greased and floured 9-x-5-x-3-inch loaf pan. Sprinkle reserved nuts and cranberries on top. Let batter rest in pan for 20 minutes on top of stove before baking. Bake at 325 degrees for 1 hour. Remove from pan to cool. May freeze if desired. Yield: 1 loaf.

Dorothy Merritt
Mid Anne Arundel Unit (Gambrills)

Early Maryland Farmers
1710

PEACH BREAD

2 1/2 cups peach purée
6 tablespoons sugar
2 cups plain flour
1 teaspoon baking soda
1 teaspoon baking
   powder
1 teaspoon ground
   cinnamon

1 cups pecans, finely
   chopped (optional)
1 teaspoon vanilla
   extract
1 1/2 cups sugar
1/2 cup margarine
2 eggs

Preheat oven to 325 degrees. Whirl fresh peaches in a blender to make purée; add 6 tablespoons of sugar; blend to mix. Set aside. Sift dry ingredients together and set aside. Cream the 1 1/2 cups sugar and margarine, add eggs and beat well. Add peaches, then dry ingredients, stirring gently until well moistened. Stir in nuts and vanilla and pour batter into two greased and floured 9-x-5-x-3 inch loaf pans. Bake at 325 degrees for 55 to 60 minutes. Cool 10 minutes in pan then turn out on rack and cool completely. Yield: 10 servings.

Evelyn Hunter
Communities United Unit

CINNAMON MUFFINS

1 1/2 cups sifted flour
1/4 cup granulated sugar
1/2 cup brown sugar
2 teaspoons baking
   powder

1/2 teaspoon salt
1/2 teaspoon cinnamon
1 egg, beaten
1/2 cup oil
1/2 cup milk

Preheat oven to 400 degrees. Grease muffin pans. Sift all dry ingredients together into a large mixing bowl. Combine egg, oil, and milk in a small bowl; add to dry ingredients. Stir just to moisten. Fill muffin pans 2/3 full. Bake for about 20 minutes. Yield: 12 muffins.
Note: May add 1/2 cup raisins to batter if desired.

Pamela F. Bilbrough
Caroline County Unit (Denton)

BUTTER BRIGHT PASTRIES

2 (¹/₄-ounce) packages
  dry yeast
¹/₄ cup warm water
¹/₃ cup sugar
¹/₈ teaspoon salt

1 cup milk
4 to 4¹/₂ cups sifted flour
2 eggs
1 cup butter or
  margarine

Dissolve yeast in warm water. Combine yeast mixture, sugar, salt and milk together. Beat in 2 cups flour; add eggs, beating well. Stir in enough flour to make a soft dough. Cover and refrigerate for 15 minutes. On a lightly floured surface, roll dough into an 18-x-15 inch rectangle. Cut ¹/₃ cup butter into small pieces. Dot surface of dough with butter, leaving a 1-inch margin. Fold 18-inch side of dough into thirds and then fold 15-inch side into thirds. Wrap in floured aluminum foil; chill 15 minutes. Remove from refrigerator and roll out dough into rectangle again. Repeat procedure twice, using remaining butter; chill for 15 minutes each time. Remove from refrigerator and divide dough into fourths. Roll out, ¹/₄ at a time and cut into desired shapes. Let rise until doubled. Bake in a preheated 400 degree oven for 8 to 10 minutes. Cool. Fill with assorted jams and jellies and glaze with the following mixture:

1 cup sifted powdered
  sugar
2 tablespoons butter

2 tablespoons evaporated
  milk
¹/₂ teaspoon vanilla

Note: These pastries are especially good served warm. To reheat, wrap in aluminum foil and heat at 400 degrees for 10 minutes.

Nancy R. Anders
Carroll County Unit (Taneytown)

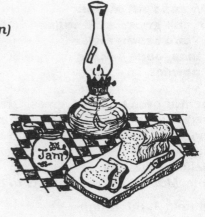

STICKY CINNAMON BUNS

1 cup milk, scalded
1/4 cup sugar
1/4 cup butter, melted
1 teaspoon salt
1 (1/4-ounce) package dry
   yeast
1/4 cup lukewarm water
1 egg, beaten
3 1/2 cups flour

4 tablespoons butter,
   melted
1/2 cup sugar
1 tablespoon cinnamon
1/2 cup raisins
1/2 cup pecans (optional)
4 tablespoons butter,
   melted
2/3 cup brown sugar

In a large bowl combine milk, sugar, butter and salt. Cool to lukewarm. Add yeast which has been softened in 1/4 cup warm water. Add egg. Gradually beat in flour. Cover and let rise in a warm place until doubled in size (about 1 hour). Turn out onto a floured surface. Knead until stickiness disappears, adding flour as needed. Roll into a rectangle about 8-x-12-x-1/4 inch thick. Brush with melted butter. Sprinkle with a mixture of the next four ingredients. Roll up lengthwise and cut into 1-inch slices with a sharp knife. Prepare two 9-inch baking pans by melting 2 tablespoons butter in each and sprinkling with 1/3 cup brown sugar. Place half the slices in each pan. Cover with a clean towel and let rise until doubled. Bake in a preheated 350 degree oven for 25 to 30 minutes or until brown. Immediately invert pan onto a plate or cookie sheet. For individual buns, cover bottom of muffin cups with melted butter and sprinkle with brown sugar, topping with one sliced bun. Proceed as above.

Note: What a great project for a winter afternoon - to bake from scratch a batch of sticky cinnamon buns! Have some to eat right away while still warm from the oven, freeze some to serve for breakfast another day, use them for great gifts for a hostess, an invalid, housewarmings, or to serve to unexpected guests for morning coffee. The recipe doubles easily.

Mrs. Walter B. Harris
Kent County Unit (Chestertown)

ALMA'S PRIZE BREAD

1/3 cup Wesson oil
2 tablespoons Grandma's
   molasses
1/3 cup light brown sugar
2 1/3 teaspoons salt
1 cup evaporated milk
1 cup hot water

1/3 cup lukewarm water
1 (1/4-ounce) package
   dry yeast
1/3 cup wheat germ
5 to 6 cups unbleached
   flour

Measure oil, molasses, brown sugar, salt, evaporated milk and hot water into a large mixing bowl. Sprinkle yeast into lukewarm water. Stir to dissolve. Stir yeast mixture into liquid mixture. Add one cup of flour with wheat germ; mix well. Stir in remaining flour until mix is stiff enough to handle. Knead about 5 minutes or until dough is "springy" to touch. Let rise in a warm place until doubled in bulk, about 1 3/4 hours. Turn onto lightly floured surface; divide dough into two equal portions and make a round ball of each. Let rest, covered, for 5 minutes. Grease two 9-x-5-x-3 inch loaf pans well. Roll each ball of dough into a rectangle. Roll sides up and press together at seam, turning under ends. Place loaves into greased pans, seam side down. Cover with cloth or wax paper; let rise in a warm place until doubled. Pans should be full with a nicely rounded top on the dough. Bake in a preheated 400 degree oven for 10 minutes; reduce heat to 325 degrees and bake for 30 minutes more. Turn out of pans and place on a cooling rack. Baked bread will sound hollow when rapped with knuckles on the bottom if it is done. Yield: 2 loaves.

Virginia Clark Waas
Annapolis Unit (Annapolis)

BEST EVER QUICK BISCUITS

1 cup self-rising flour
2 tablespoons mayonnaise

1/2 cup milk

Preheat oven to 425 degrees. Combine all ingredients and drop into 7 greased muffin cups. Bake at 425 degrees for 20 minutes. Yield: 7 biscuits.
Note: 1 cup plain flour, 1 1/2 teaspoons baking powder, and 1/4 teaspoon salt may be substituted for 1 cup self-rising flour.

Michele Ryan
Bowie/Oxon Hill Unit (Bowie)

STRAWBERRY BREAD

3 cups flour
1 teaspoon salt
1 teaspoon soda
1 tablespoon cinnamon
2 cups sugar
3 eggs, well-beaten

1 1/4 cups salad oil
2 (10-ounce) packages
   frozen, sliced
   strawberries, thawed
   and drained
1 1/4 cups chopped pecans

Combine flour, salt, soda, cinnamon and sugar. Make a well in the center of the dry ingredients; add eggs and oil, stirring only until dry ingredients are moistened. Stir in strawberries and pecans. Spoon batter into two lightly greased 9-x-5-x-3 inch loaf pans. Bake at 350 degrees for 1 hour or until bread tests done. Let stand overnight before slicing. Yield: 2 loaves.

Mrs. Ronald H. Peele, Sr. (Judy)
Severna Park Unit (Severna Park)

BONNACK
("SHORT" IRISH BREAKFAST BREAD)

3 cups all purpose flour
1 1/2 teaspoons baking soda
1 1/2 teaspoons salt
1/4 cup butter or
   margarine

1 cup seedless raisins
Buttermilk
1 tablespoon sugar

Preheat oven to 350 degrees. Grease and flour a 9-inch cake pan. Place unsifted flour into a large mixing bowl; add baking soda and salt. Mix lightly with a fork. Coarsely cut up butter and drop into flour mixture. With hands or a pastry cutter, mix until the consistency of crumbs. Add raisins. Using a fork, mix in enough buttermilk to reach a drop biscuit consistency (not too wet). Heap batter into the middle of the cake pan, keeping about 1 inch from the sides. Sprinkle the top with sugar. Bake for 45 minutes or until cake tester or toothpick inserted in center comes out clean. Empty Bonnack onto a clean kitchen towel, wrap, turn right side up and cool on a wire rack.
Note: Keep refrigerated or frozen until ready to use. Excellent toasted for breakfast!

Helen Marquiss
Towson Unit (Towson)

BARBARA'S FAVORITE ITALIAN BREAD

1 (¼-ounce) package
dry yeast
1½ teaspoons salt

2 cups lukewarm water
5 cups flour
Sugar

Dissolve yeast in ¼ cup warm water, add a pinch of sugar. After the yeast has begun to work, add it to remaining 1¾ cups water in a large mixing bowl. Stir in the salt. Add flour, ½ to 1 cup at a time. Continue to stir in flour until dough pulls away from the sides of the bowl. Turn dough out on a floured surface; knead for about 8 minutes or until smooth and elastic, kneading in as much flour as the dough will hold. Place the dough into a lightly greased bowl, turn to grease top and sides, cover with a damp cloth and let rise for 1½ to 2 hours or until doubled. After first rising, punch down dough and knead it in the bowl a few times, cover and let rise until doubled again. After rising, punch dough down, turn out onto a clean surface and knead once or twice; let rest for 5 minutes. Cut dough in half and form two loaves by flattening out the dough and then tightly rolling it up, jelly-roll fashion, from one of the edges. Place loaves onto a greased cookie sheet, let rise until doubled ½ hour, slash diagonally a few times, then let rise another ½ hour. Bake at 400 degrees for 50 minutes.

Carl H. Burkhart
Lanham/Bowie Unit (Bowie)

SOUTHERN CORN MUFFINS
(WITH MY OWN SPECIAL TOUCH!)

2 cups cornmeal (Indian
Head Stone Ground-
yellow or white)
1½ teaspoons salt
2 cups boiling water
½ cup sugar

1 cup milk
2 eggs
2 tablespoons butter,
melted
4 teaspoons baking
powder

Preheat oven to 475 degrees. Mix cornmeal and salt. Gradually stir in water. Stir until smooth. Stir in the sugar; then milk, eggs and butter; add baking powder; stir. Pour into well-greased muffin cups, an 8-inch square pan or a 15-x-10-x-1 inch biscuit pan. Bake at 475 degrees for 25 minutes.

Mrs. Elois Reynolds
Somerset County Unit (Princess Anne)

FRENCH BREAKFAST PUFFS

1/3 cup soft shortening
1/2 cup sugar
1 egg, slightly beaten
1 1/2 cups sifted flour
1 1/2 teaspoons baking
    powder
1/4 teaspoon nutmeg

1/2 teaspoon salt
1/2 cup milk
6 tablespoons melted
    butter or margarine
1/2 cup sugar
1 teaspoon cinnamon

Mix shortening, sugar and egg. Sift flour, baking powder, nutmeg and salt together. Stir dry ingredients into shortening mixture alternately with milk. Fill small muffin cups 2/3 full and bake 20 to 25 minutes at 350 degrees. Mix sugar and cinnamon together in a small bowl. Dip hot puffs quickly into melted butter and then into sugar/cinnamon mixture. These may be made ahead and reheated at the last minute. These puffs also freeze well. Yield: 24

Mary Burgess
Anne Arundel County - South County Unit (Davidsonville)
Similar recipe submitted by: Marilyn Senn
St. Mary's County Unit (Lexington Park)

CHEESY MOON BREAD

3/4 cup warm water
1 box hot roll mix
1 egg
1 tablespoon butter
1 1/2 teaspoon garlic salt

1/2 teaspoon ground basil
1/2 teaspoon oregano
1/2 teaspoon paprika
1/2 cup Parmesan cheese
1/2 cup olives, chopped

Grease a 12-inch pizza pan well. In a mixing bowl combine warm water with yeast. Stir in butter, egg and seasonings. Add prepared hot roll mix, olives and cheese. Stir, cover, and let rise in a warm place for 30 to 45 minutes. Turn dough out onto a well-floured surface and knead about 10 times. Shape dough into a 12-inch round and place on a greased pizza pan. Cover and let rise until doubled. Slit top 3 or 4 times. Brush with a beaten egg, if desired. Bake in a preheated 325 degree oven for 40 to 45 minutes.
Note: Great with Italian dishes!

Becky Coleman
Dorchester County Unit (Vienna)

GERMAN DARK RYE BREAD

3 cups sifted all-purpose
 flour
2 (¼-ounce) packages
 dry yeast
¼ cup cocoa powder
1 tablespoon caraway
 seed

2 cups water
⅓ cup molasses
2 tablespoons butter
1 tablespoon sugar
1 tablespoon salt
3 to 3½ cups rye flour

Soften yeast in ¼ cup lukewarm water. In a large mixing bowl combine the all-purpose flour, cocoa and caraway seed. In a saucepan, combine remaining 1¾ cups water, molasses, butter, sugar and salt; heat until warm, stirring to melt butter. Add to dry ingredients. Beat at a low speed with an electric mixer for ½ minute, scraping sides of bowl constantly. Beat 3 minutes at high speed. By hand, stir in enough rye flour to make a soft dough. Turn onto a floured surface. Knead until smooth (8 to 10 minutes), using more flour as needed. Place in a greased bowl; turn to grease both sides of dough. Cover and place in a warm area to rise until doubled (approximately 1½ hours). Punch dough down and divide in half. Shape each half into a round loaf, brush surface of loaves with a little oil. Place on greased baking sheet or in two 8" pie pans. Slash 3 cuts across top of loaves with a sharp knife. Let rise until double (about 1 hour). Bake in a preheated 400 degree oven for 25 to 30 minutes. Remove from pans to cool. Yield: 2 loaves.

Marilyn Senn
St. Mary's County Unit (Lexington Park)

SIXTY MINUTE ROLLS

1½ cups warm water
2 tablespoons shortening
2 tablespoons sugar
1 (¼-ounce) package
 dry yeast

¼ cup lukewarm water
1 egg
1 teaspoon salt
4 cups flour

Dissolve yeast in ¼ cup warm water. Stir all ingredients together with a spoon. Let rise 15 minutes; punch down and let rise 15 minutes longer. Shape into rolls and let rise 15 minutes more. Bake in a 400 degree oven for 15 minutes or until brown. Makes 12 rolls.

Victoria Fleet
Marlboro/Aquasco Unit (Brandywine)

SIMPSON'S SUMPTUOUS SOUTHERN ROLLS

5 teaspoons sugar
2 teaspoons salt
1 (¼-ounce) package dry
yeast
6 to 7 cups flour

1 tablespoon Crisco
shortening
2 cups water
(approximately)

Combine the yeast, 1 teaspoon sugar, and 1 cup lukewarm water; let stand for 10 minutes. Combine 4 teaspoons sugar, 2 teaspoons salt, shortening, and 2 cups flour in a large bowl. Stir in yeast mixture. Beat in remaining flour and water until mixture leaves sides of bowl. Turn out onto floured surface and knead a few times. Roll into a ball; place in a greased bowl; turn to grease both sides. Place in a warm place to double in bulk, about 5 hours. Punch dough down and roll into golf-ball size balls. Place on a greased baking pan and brush tops with melted shortening. Place in a warm spot to rise until doubled, about 3 hours. Bake at 350 degrees until brown (about 8 to 10 minutes).
Note: These rolls are best made in the morning for dinner. They're delicious fried as fritters for breakfast instead of baking.

James C. Simpson
Northern Charles County Unit (Waldorf)

HERNDON'S BUTTER DIPS

⅓ cup butter, melted
2½ cups sifted flour
1 teaspoon sugar
3½ teaspoons baking
powder

1½ teaspoons salt
1 cup milk

Heat oven to 450 degrees and melt butter in an 8-inch square baking pan. While butter is melting, mix remaining ingredients in a bowl. Turn mixture out of bowl onto a lightly floured surface and knead ten times. Roll out ½-inch thick with a rolling pin to fit the baking pan. Cut the dough in half lengthwise, then in equal portions widthwise eight times (16 rolls). Take each roll and dip in melted butter to cover. Place in pan. Bake for 15 to 20 minutes or until golden brown. Yield: 16 rolls.

Donna Herndon
Montgomery County Unit (Brookville)

POTATO ROLLS

½ cup sugar
1 cup warm, mashed
   potatoes, cooked with 2
   teaspoons salt*
½ cup shortening
1 egg, beaten

1 (¼-ounce) package dry
   yeast
1 cup warm water (potato
   water may be used)
8 cups flour

Combine sugar, potatoes, shortening, and egg in a large bowl. Dissolve yeast in warm water in small bowl; add to potato mixture. Mix in about 4 cups of the flour to make a stiff dough. Knead in remaining flour and continue kneading until dough is smooth and elastic. Place dough in a well-greased bowl and turn once to grease the top. Cover and let dough rise in a warm, draft-free area until doubled in bulk (about 1½ hours). Punch dough down and shape into rolls or a loaf. Place in pan, cover, and let rise again until doubled in size. Preheat oven to 400 degrees and bake 12 to 15 minutes for rolls, 30 to 45 minutes for loaf.
*Instant potatoes may be used.

Mrs. Amos E. Lang (Betty)
Wicomico County Unit (Salisbury)

HOT ROLLS

2 (¼-ounce) packages
   dry yeast
¼ cup sugar
¼ cup lukewarm water
1 cup milk

1 tablespoon salt
1 tablespoon margarine
1 egg, beaten
4½ cups flour

Dissolve yeast and sugar in lukewarm water. Scald milk, remove from heat and add salt and margarine. Add warm milk mixture and egg to the yeast mixture. Stir well. Stir in flour until dough leaves sides of the bowl; turn out onto well-floured surface and knead 8 to 10 minutes or until smooth. Grease top with margarine. Cover and let rise until doubled in bulk (about 1 hour). Punch dough down. Turn out onto a lightly floured surface and shape into rolls as desired. Cover; let rise until doubled in bulk (30 to 60 minutes). Bake in a preheated 400 degree oven for 10 to 15 minutes. Yield: 3 dozen rolls.

Mrs. Ruth R. Briscoe
Kent County Unit (Worton)

Cakes

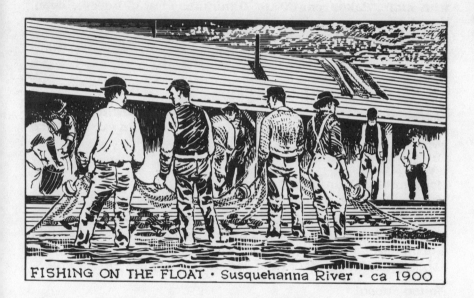

FISHING ON THE FLOAT · Susquehanna River · ca 1900

Float Fishing—Don Kimball
Susquehanna River © 1900. Lower Susquehanna was once the
site of large floating fishing factories employing many people.

FRESH COCONUT POUND CAKE

2 cups butter	4 cups sifted all-purpose
4 cups powdered sugar	flour
6 eggs	1/2 teaspoon salt
2 teaspoons vanilla	1 cup fresh grated coconut

Cream butter, beat in sugar gradually until well blended. Add eggs, one at a time; add vanilla. Gradually beat in combined flour and salt until well blended. Add fresh coconut, stir in well. Spread in buttered, floured 12-cup bundt pan. Cut through batter with knife. Bake from 60 to 70 minutes in a 350 degree oven. Cool in pan on wire rack for 15 minutes. Invert onto rack and cool completely. Makes one 10-inch cake.
Note: Do not substitute ingredients.

Mrs. Gladys Gardner
Howard County Unit (Ellicott City)
Variation: Glaze for coconut cake: 1/4 cup water and 1/4 cup sugar boiled for 1 minute; add 1 teaspoon vanilla extract. Drizzle over cake while still warm.

Carole Mattis
Montgomery County Unit (Gaithersburg)
Variation: For Southern Coconut Pound Cake: 3 cups sugar, 1 cup butter, 3 cups unbleached flour, 1 teaspoon baking powder, 1/2 teaspoon salt, 1 cup milk, 1 tablespoon lemon juice, 5 eggs, 1 cup unsweetened coconut. Use same mixing procedure for cake above. Bake in bundt or tube pan at 300 degrees for 1 1/2 hours.

Nancy Pascal
Anne Arundel County Unit (Severna Park)

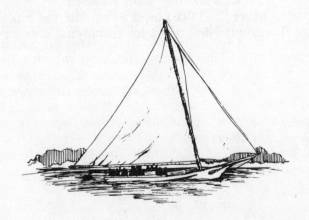

WACKY CHOCOLATE CAKE

3 tablespoons cocoa
1½ cups flour
1 cup sugar
1 teaspoon baking powder
1 scant teaspoon baking
  soda

½ teaspoon salt
1 tablespoon vinegar
1 teaspoon vanilla
5 tablespoons shortening
1 cup very hot water

Sift all dry ingredients into an ungreased 13-x-9-x3-inch pan. Make 3 holes in the dry mix. Into one hole place 1 tablespoon vinegar; in another, place 1 teaspoon vanilla; and in the third, 5 tablespoons shortening. Pour 1 cup very hot water over shortening and stir mixture until smooth. Bake at 350 degrees for about 30 minutes.

Betty Rimpo
Dorchester County Unit (Cambridge)

BEST EVER COFFEE CAKE

3 cups sifted flour
1 tablespoon baking
  powder
1 teaspoon salt
1 cup soft shortening
1 cup granulated sugar
2 eggs, unbeaten
1 cup milk
1 teaspoon vanilla
1½ cups light brown sugar

3 tablespoons flour
2½ to 3 tablespoons
  cinnamon
¾ cup melted butter or
  margarine
1½ cups raisins, rinsed in
  hot water
1½ cups coarsely chopped
  walnuts

Preheat oven to 350 degrees. Grease bottoms of two 8-x-8-x-2-inch pans. Sift the first 3 ingredients. Cream shortening with sugar and eggs until very light and fluffy. (Medium speed if using electric mixer.) Mix in alternately, just until smooth, flour mixture in fourths and combined milk and vanilla in thirds. Spread ¼ batter in each pan; top with ¼ of combined brown sugar, 3 tablespoons flour, and cinnamon; pour on ¼ of melted butter; then sprinkle with ¼ of the raisins and nuts. Repeat layers. Bake 50 minutes at 350 degrees. Makes 16 to 20 servings.
Note: Cake may also be baked in a 13-x-9-x-2 inch pan for 50 minutes or until done.

Myra Hettleman
Northwest Community Unit (Baltimore)

GOLDEN FRUITCAKE

2 cups red candied
  cherries
1 cup diced candied lemon
  peel
1 cup diced candied orange
  peel
1 cup diced candied
  pineapple wedges
1 (10-ounce) container
  pitted dates, sliced
2 cups golden raisins
1 cup California walnuts,
  chopped
3³/₄ cups all-purpose flour,
  divided

2 cups sugar
1 cup butter or margarine,
  softened
6 eggs
1 cup cream sherry
2 teaspoons double-acting
  baking powder
¹/₂ teaspoon salt
2 whole angelica* for
  garnish
2 tablespoons lemon juice
  (approximately)
2 cups powdered sugar

Preheat oven to 300 degrees. Line a 10-inch tube pan with foil. Cut cherries in half. Reserve 15 halves for garnish. In large bowl combine remaining cherries, next 6 ingredients and ³/₄ cup flour. In another large bowl, with mixer at medium speed, beat sugar and butter until fluffy. Add eggs, sherry, baking powder, salt, and remaining flour. Beat at low speed until mixed. Beat 4 minutes at medium speed. Stir in fruit mixture. Spoon batter into pan. Bake 3 hours until toothpick inserted in center comes out clean. Cool on rack; remove from pan and peel off foil. Wrap tightly with plastic wrap. Refrigerate cake up to 2 months. To serve: Cut angelica into 15 leaves. In small bowl, stir lemon juice, a little at a time, into powdered sugar until spreading consistency; garnish cake with glaze, leaves and reserved cherry halves. Makes one 7-pound fruit cake.

*Candy used to cut leaves and stem for decoration.

Eileen M. Cohen
Northwest Community Unit (Randallstown)

PUMPKIN CHOCOLATE CHIP CAKE

2 cups all-purpose flour
2 cups sugar
4 eggs
2 teaspoons baking powder
2 teaspoons baking soda
1/2 teaspoon salt

1/2 teaspoon cinnamon
1 cup vegetable oil
2 cups solid-pack pumpkin
1 cup chocolate chips
1 cup chopped nuts
  (optional)

Mix all ingredients together with a spoon. Pour into an ungreased 10-inch tube pan or two 9-x-5-x-3 inch ungreased loaf pans. Bake at 350 degrees for 1 hour and 15 minutes. This makes a fabulous dessert for the cook in a hurry. No mixer, no mess, no fuss! Be sure to leave the pans ungreased.

Mrs. Bernardine Ginsberg
Northwest Community Unit (Baltimore)

DUMP CAKE

1 (20-ounce) can crushed
  pineapple, undrained
1 (20-ounce) can cherry
  pie filling (or fruit
  filling of your choice)

1 package white or yellow
  cake mix
1 cup chopped walnuts
1 stick butter or
  margarine

Dump the pie filling in an ungreased 9-x-13-x-2 inch rectangular pan. Dump the pineapple over the pie filling followed by the cake mix. Spread evenly. Sprinkle the walnuts over the cake mix. Cut the butter into small pieces and spread over the mixture. Bake at 350 degrees for 55 minutes.
Note: If top is not crispy brown turn oven up to 400 and bake for another 10 minutes.

Sarah H. Jolley
Dorchester County Unit (Vienna)
Jackie Wilkins
Communities United Unit

APPLE CAKE

3 cups diced or thinly
   sliced apples
2 cups sugar
1 cup Wesson oil
2 eggs, well beaten
2 teaspoons vanilla

3 cups flour
1 teaspoon baking soda
½ teaspoon salt
1 teaspoon cinnamon
½ cup nuts
½ cup raisins

Mix together the first 5 ingredients. Stir in the remaining ingredients. Pour into a sheet cake pan and bake at 350 degrees for 45 minutes. When almost cool, sprinkle with sifted powdered sugar.

Janie H. Saddler
Queen Annes County Unit (Grasonville)
Variation: Blend ⅓ cup melted butter and ½ cup brown sugar and spoon over slightly warm cake.

Anne R. Allen
Mid-Anne Arundel Unit (Crofton)
Variation: Add ½ cup orange juice to cake batter.

Susan Towers
Caroline County (Denton)

EASIEST-EVER CAKE

1 cup milk
¹/₂ cup butter
4 eggs
2 cups sugar

2 cups all-purpose flour
2 teaspoons baking powder
¹/₂ teaspoon salt
1 teaspoon vanilla

Melt butter in milk. Beat eggs well. Add sugar to eggs and beat *very* well. Mix flour, baking powder and salt together; add to egg mixture, and beat well. Add milk and butter mixture and vanilla. Pour into greased and floured 10-inch tube pan. Bake in 350-degree oven for 50 to 55 minutes or until toothpick inserted in cake comes out clean.

Margie Freedenberg
Montgomery County Unit (Silver Spring)

BLACK WALNUT CAKE

1 cup butter
1 pound box powdered
 sugar
5 eggs, beaten
1 teaspoon vanilla
1 cup chopped black
 walnuts

3 cups flour
1 teaspoon baking powder
¹/₂ teaspoon salt
1 cup milk

Cream butter and sugar until creamy. Add beaten eggs and vanilla. Beat until blended with mixer. Add black walnuts; mix well. Sift together flour, baking powder and salt. Stir into creamed mixture alternately with milk, starting and ending with flour. Grease and flour a tube pan. Bake at 350 degrees for 1 hour.

Flo Horney
Queen Annes County Unit (Centreville)

LEMON SPICE LOAF

1 (7-ounce) package
gingerbread mix
1 (7-ounce) package lemon
cake mix

1 cup water, divided
³/₄ cup raisins
³/₄ cup nuts (optional)

Preheat oven to 375 degrees. Grease loaf pan (9-x-5-x-3 inch) generously and dust with flour. Empty gingerbread and lemon cake mixes into medium bowl. Blend in ¹/₂ cup water. Beat with electric mixer at medium speed for 2 minutes. Blend in remaining ¹/₂ cup water and beat an additional minute. Add raisins to batter. Sprinkle with nuts and bake 20 to 25 minutes. Cool about 10 minutes. Serve with your favorite topping. Serves 6.

Gertrude Shockley
Wicomico County Unit (Salisbury)

BLUEBERRY ROLL

1¹/₂ cups flour, sifted
2 teaspoons baking
powder
¹/₂ teaspoon salt
2 tablespoons sugar

5 tablespoons shortening
1 egg
¹/₄ cup milk
1¹/₂ cup fresh blueberries
¹/₂ cup sugar

Combine flour, baking powder, salt and sugar; sift into bowl. With two knives or pastry blender, cut in shortening until mixture resembles coarse cornmeal. With fork, beat egg slightly; add milk to make ¹/₂ cup in all; blend well. Add to flour mixture and stir quickly with fork until just mixed. Turn out on floured board. With floured fingertips, knead gently about 10 times, until outside looks smooth. Roll or pat into rectangle about 8 by 10 inches. Cover dough evenly with blueberries except for 1 inch on both long sides. Sprinkle ¹/₂ cup sugar over berries. Starting at 1 long side, roll up like a jelly roll. Place in greased, shallow baking pan (about 11 by 7 inches). Bake at 400 degrees until golden brown, about 40 to 45 minutes. Cut in slices and serve warm with cream. Yield: 6 servings.
Note: If using frozen berries, do not thaw first.

Ruth Lichtenberger
Kent County Unit (Chestertown)

7-UP CAKE (DIABETIC)

4 eggs
1/2 cup cooking oil
1 (3-3/4 ounce) box lemon
   instant pudding mix
1 box cake mix

1 teaspoon salt
1 tablespoon lemon
   extract
1 small bottle 7-Up

Put all ingredients in large bowl and beat for 5 minutes, mixing thoroughly. Grease and flour a tube pan and bake at 375 degrees for 45 to 50 minutes. Let cool 5 minutes; turn onto rack to complete cooling.

Mrs. Ruth Collick
Worcester County Unit (Girdletree)

POUND CAKE DELIGHT
WITH TANGY LEMON GLAZE

3 cups sifted flour
1 teaspoon baking
   powder
1/2 teaspoon salt
1 cup butter
1/2 cup shortening

3 cups sugar
6 eggs
1 1/2 teaspoons rum extract
1 teaspoon lemon extract
1 cup milk

Sift together flour, baking powder, and salt. Cream together butter, shortening and sugar until light and airy. Add eggs, 1 at a time, beating well after each addition. Add extracts. Beat for a total of 10 minutes. Add dry ingredients alternately with milk, beating well after each addition. Pour batter into greased and floured 10-inch tube pan. Bake in a 325 degree oven for 1 1/2 hours or until cake tests done. Cool in pan on rack for 15 minutes. Remove from pan, cool on rack.

Glaze:
Combine 1/2 cup sugar and 1/4 cup water in small pan. Bring mixture to a boil, stirring constantly. Boil 2 minutes. Stir in 1/4 teaspoon lemon extract. Place cake bottom side up on serving plate. Punch holes in top of cake with meat fork. Spoon glaze over cake. Makes 12 servings.

Mrs. D. Regina Warren
Carroll County Unit (Westminster)

HIDDEN GOLD (OR CARROT CAKE)

2 cups sugar
2 cups all-purpose flour,
  sifted
1 teaspoon salt
2 teaspoons baking soda

1 cup vegetable oil
4 eggs
3 cups raw carrots, grated
Lemon frosting
Nuts, chopped

Sift together dry ingredients; add oil and mix well. Add eggs, 1 at a time, beating well after each addition. Stir in carrots. Divide batter equally among 3 greased and floured 8-inch layer cake pans (or two 9-inch ones). Bake at 350 degrees for 35 minutes or until cake tests done. Remove from oven and cool thoroughly. Fill and top with lemon frosting; garnish with nuts.
Note: Use canned, ready-to-spread lemon frosting or packaged lemon frosting mix.

Elois B. Reynolds
Somerset County Unit (Princess Anne)

Variation: Cream Cheese Frosting: 1 (16-ounce) package powdered sugar, 1 (8-ounce) package cream cheese, softened, 1/2 cup butter or margarine, softened, 1 teaspoon vanilla extract. Cream ingredients together until well blended and spread between layers of carrot cake and on top of cake.
Note: I use 2 layers for my cake and freeze the third. Cut the third layer in half and frost with the remaining frosting. Frosting can also be frozen for future use.

Wanda L. Jackson
Cecil County Unit (Elkton)

Variation: Glaze for carrot cake: 1 cup granulated sugar, 1/2 cup buttermilk, 1/2 teaspoon baking soda, 1 tablespoon light corn syrup. Boil to soft ball stage. Stir constantly while cooking. Pour over cake immediately after removing from oven. Allow cake to sit 3 to 4 hours before removing from pan.

Mrs. Mabel B. Wilkinson
Northwest Merle-Duvall Unit (Hyattsville)

APPLESAUCE CAKE

2 cups sugar
1/2 cup shortening
2 eggs
1 1/2 cups applesauce
2 1/2 cups sifted flour
1/2 teaspoon salt,
   cinnamon, cloves,
   allspice

1 cup raisins
1/2 cup walnuts
2 teaspoons baking soda
1/2 cup boiling water

Cream shortening; add sugar. Blend in eggs and applesauce. Sift flour; add salt and spices. Mix 2 tablespoons flour with raisins and nuts. Dissolve soda in boiling water. Then add dry ingredients to the creamed mixture alternately with soda-water mixture and stir in floured raisins and nuts. Pour into a well greased and floured tube pan. Bake at 350 degrees for 1 hour.

Note: Because of the richness of this cake, the top browns before the cake is thoroughly baked. Test it thoroughly before removing from oven. Decorate cake with maraschino cherries and walnut halves.

Ann Weisenmiller
Carroll County Unit (Hempstead)
Estelle Shank
Frederick County Unit (Frederick)

1-2-3-4 CAKE

1 cup butter
2 cups sugar
3 cups sifted flour
4 eggs
1 tablespoon baking
   powder

1/2 teaspoon salt
1 cup milk
1 teaspoon vanilla

Cream butter and sugar until light. Add beaten eggs, one at a time, beating after each addition. Sift and add dry ingredients alternately with milk and flavoring. Bake in 3 greased layer cake pans in a moderately hot oven (350 to 375 degrees) about 25 to 30 minutes.

Sandra W. Younger
Calvert County Unit (St. Leonard)

HARVEST CAKE

4 cups diced apples
2 cups sugar
3 cups flour
1 cup cooking oil
2 eggs, beaten
1 cup chopped nuts

2 teaspoons baking soda
1 teaspoon salt
1 teaspoon cinnamon
1 teaspoon nutmeg
1 teaspoon vanilla

Pour sugar over diced apples and let stand for 1 hour. Add remaining ingredients, mix well. Bake at 350 degrees for 1 hour and 10 to 15 minutes.

Polly R. Whaley
Talbot County Unit (Easton)
Priscilla Teeter
Carroll County Unit (Westminster)
Mary Acree
Caroline County Unit (Ridgely)

CHOCOLATE COOKIE SHEET CAKE

$1/2$ cup margarine
$1/2$ cup Crisco oil
$6^1/2$ tablespoons cocoa, divided
1 cup water
2 cups flour
2 cups sugar
2 eggs, beaten

$1/2$ cup buttermilk
1 teaspoon soda
2 teaspoons vanilla, divided
6 tablespoons milk
1 box powdered sugar
1 cup chopped pecans

Combine margarine, oil, 5 tablespoons cocoa, and water and bring to a boil. Pour over flour and sugar which has been sifted together. Mix well and add eggs, buttermilk, 1 teaspoon vanilla, and soda. Pour on greased cookie sheet. Bake 15 to 20 minutes at 400 degrees. While cake is cooking, mix $1^1/2$ tablespoons cocoa and 6 tablespoons milk. Bring to boil. Remove and add powdered sugar while still hot, plus 1 teaspoon vanilla and 1 cup chopped pecans. After cake has cooled 5 minutes, pour over cake. Serves 20 to 30.
Note: The older this cake gets the better it tastes. Icing sinks into cake and gives it a "brownie" type texture.

Jane McCauley
Kent County Unit (Chestertown)

FUDGE CAKE

3 cups sugar
3/4 cup butter
6 eggs
1 1/2 cups cake flour
Pinch of salt

4 1/2 tablespoons cocoa
1 teaspoon vanilla
1 cup chopped (finely)
  pecans

Cream butter and sugar. Add beaten eggs 2 at a time. Sift dry ingredients together, then beat into creamed mixture. Add vanilla and stir in nuts. Bake in 2 greased and floured 11-by-7 inch aluminum pans at 300 degrees for about 50 minutes. Test with a toothpick; take out when a bit still adheres to the stick. Cut immediately into 24 pieces. Remove from pan *after* it cools.

Mrs. Dorothy Dick
Kent County Unit (Chestertown)

MEXICAN WEDDING CAKE

1 (20-ounce) can crushed
  pineapple, undrained
2 cups sugar
2 cups flour
1 teaspoon baking soda

1/4 teaspoon salt
2 teaspoons vanilla
2 eggs
1 cup chopped pecans

Combine all ingredients in a large bowl and mix well. Bake 45 to 50 minutes at 350 degrees.
Icing:

1 (8-ounce) package
  cream cheese
1/3 cup butter

1 1/2 cups powdered sugar
2 teaspoons vanilla

Mix together and spread on cooled cake.

Mrs. Shirley Mullican
Frederick County Unit (Frederick)

CHOCOLATE POUND CAKE

1 cup butter or margarine	3 cups flour
½ cup shortening	1 teaspoon baking
3 cups sugar	powder
5 eggs	¼ teaspoon salt
1 cup milk	5 tablespoons cocoa
1 teaspoon vanilla	

Cream butter and shortening with sugar until fluffy. Add eggs 1 at a time; add milk and vanilla. Sift dry ingredients and add to creamed mixture. Pour into a greased tube pan and bake 1 hour and 10 minutes at 300 degrees.

Mrs. Eleanor O'Donnell
Frederick County Unit (Frederick)

SHERRY WINE CAKE

1 package yellow cake	4 eggs
mix	1 cup cooking oil
1 package instant	1 cup sherry wine
butterscotch pudding	1 ounce poppy seeds

Mix all ingredients together and beat 5 minutes. Pour into greased and floured tube pan. Bake at 350 degrees for 55 to 60 minutes. Leave plain or sprinkle with powdered sugar after removing from oven.

Martha B. Schmidt
Talbot County Unit (Easton)

CORNSTARCH FROSTING

1 cup water	1 cup granulated sugar
3 tablespoons cornstarch	1 tablespoon vanilla
1 cup butter or margarine	

Mix water and cornstarch together and cook until thick; set aside to cool. Cream butter, sugar and vanilla together; add to cooled cornstarch mixture. Beat with electric mixer until it looks like whipped cream. This will frost a 2 layer (9-inch) cake.

Kitty Walters
Southwest Baltimore City Unit (Baltimore)

MAYONNAISE CAKE

2 cups flour
1 cup sugar
5 tablespoons cocoa
2 teaspoons baking soda

1/2 teaspoon salt
1 cup mayonnaise
1 cup cold coffee
1 teaspoon vanilla

Sift flour, sugar, cocoa, baking soda and salt together; then add mayonnaise, coffee and vanilla to dry ingredients, mix well. Pour batter into greased and floured 13-x-9-inch pan. Bake at 350 degrees for 20 to 30 minutes until done. Frost with favorite icing or peanut butter icing is very good.
Note: Cake is dark chocolate and a good keeper.

Mrs. Sandra J. Cain
Northern Charles County Unit (Waldorf)

SKILLET CAKE

1 package yellow cake mix

Mix according to directions on package. Pour batter into an electric skillet which has been greased with cooking oil and heated to 275 degrees. Bake 22 minutes and then turn off heat, open vent and add topping.

Topping:

Grated rind of 1/2 orange
1/2 cup brown sugar
1 1/2 teaspoons cinnamon
1/4 cup graham cracker
  crumbs

2 tablespoons melted
  butter
1/2 cup chopped nuts

Mix and spread evenly on baked cake. Return lid to skillet and let stand 10 minutes. Cake may be served hot or cold. Leave lid off after the 10 minute waiting period.

Mrs. Catherine Yocum
Allegany County Unit (Rawlings)

EASY APPLE PIE CAKE

2 tablespoons margarine
1 cup sugar
1 egg, beaten
1 cup flour
1 teaspoon baking soda

Pinch of salt
1 tablespoon hot water
4 apples, sliced thin
Nuts
Whipped topping

Cream margarine and sugar. Add beaten egg, flour, soda, salt, hot water and sliced apples. Mix until well blended. Pour into ungreased pie pan. Sprinkle with nuts. Bake approximately 35 minutes at 350 degrees. Serve with whipped topping.
Note: If apples are large, use only 3 or it may run over. Don't forget the whipped topping; it tastes so much better when you add that finishing touch.

Mrs. Claire LeCompte
Severna Park Unit (Severna Park)

CREAM CHEESE CAKE

1 pound cream cheese,
    softened
3 eggs
²/₃ cup sugar
¹/₂ teaspoon almond
    extract

1 cup sour cream
3 tablespoons sugar
1 teaspoon vanilla

Beat softened cream cheese, eggs; add sugar and almond extract. Beat until smooth, thick and lemon colored. Pour into greased (10-x6-inch) Pyrex dish and bake in a preheated 350 degree oven for 25 minutes. Cool 20 minutes. While cake is cooling, beat sour cream, 3 tablespoons sugar and vanilla together. Pour evenly over top of cheesecake and return to oven and bake 10 minutes more.

Mrs. Maryland Massey
Kent County Unit (Millington)
JoAnne E. Bayles
Montgomery County Unit (Rockville)

PUMPKIN PIE CAKE

1 (18-ounce) box yellow
   cake mix (reserve 1 cup
   for topping)
1/2 cup margarine
1 egg
2 cups pumpkin
3 eggs
2/3 cup milk

1/2 cup brown sugar
1 teaspoon cinnamon
1/2 teaspoon ginger
1/2 teaspoon nutmeg
1 cup cake mix (reserved
   from above)
1/2 cup sugar
1/4 cup margarine

Mix cake mix, margarine, and egg; press into greased and floured
13-x-9-x-2 inch pan. Mix together the pumpkin, 3 eggs, milk,
brown sugar and spices; pour over first layer. Mix the reserved
cake mix, 1/2 cup sugar and 1/4 margarine into a crumb mixture;
sprinkle over layers already in pan. Bake at 350 degrees for 45 to
60 minutes or until done.
Note: Recipe also works well with white or spice cake mix.

J. Lynn Daugherty
Frederick County Unit (Frederick)

Fort McHenry & Harbor

STRAWBERRY ANGEL FOOD CAKE MOLD

1 small angel food cake
1 small box frozen
  strawberries

1 large box strawberry-
  flavored gelatin (use
  only 2 cups hot water)

Use Par-T-Fel Tupperware mold with tube. Grease mold lightly. Mix gelatin and strawberries together. Pour some of mixture in mold, then put the angel food cake in mold over the tube. Puncture the cake with a knife in several places, pour some of the mixture in these places, along edges and over cake. Place top on cake and refrigerate until firm about 4 hours. Take tube part out first and holding cake over a plate, shake free from mold.

Helen T. Daniels
South Potomac Unit (Suitland)

Desserts

Annapolis Capitol Dome—Harriet Reichard
Annapolis is the state capitol of Maryland, the home of the U.S. Naval Academy and the heartland of many sailors. It is a truly beautiful waterfront city.

ITALIAN ANISE COOKIES

2 cups granulated sugar
1 cup butter or
margarine, melted
1/4 cup anise seed
1 teaspoon anise extract
3 tablespoons bourbon or
2 teaspoons vanilla
extract and 2
tablespoons water

2 cups chopped almonds
or walnuts
6 eggs
5 1/2 cups flour (all-purpose)
1 tablespoon baking
powder

Preheat oven to 375 degrees. Mix sugar with butter, anise seed, extracts and nuts. Beat in eggs. Sift and measure flour with baking powder into sugar mixture. Blend thoroughly. Cover and chill 2 to 3 hours. May be refrigerated overnight. On a lightly floured board, shape dough with your hands to form 6 flat loaves that are about 1/2 inch thick and 2 inches wide and as long as the cookie sheets. Place on greased cookie sheets. Bake for 20 minutes. Remove from oven and cool, until you can touch them. Cut diagonal slices about 1/2 to 3/4 inch thick. Lay slices on cookie sheets close together and return to oven (375 degrees) for 15 minutes or until lightly toasted. Cool on wire rack and store in air tight container. Makes 9 dozen.

Mrs. William F. Bergeron
Northern Baltimore County Unit (Phoenix)

RUSSIAN TEA COOKIES

1 cup butter or margarine
1/2 cup powdered sugar
1 teaspoon vanilla
2 1/4 cups sifted all-purpose
flour

1/4 teaspoon salt
3/4 cup finely chopped
nuts

Preheat oven to 400 degrees. Cream butter and sugar; add vanilla, flour, salt, nuts; mix well. Form into dime-sized balls, or flatten if preferred. Place on ungreased baking sheet. Bake for 12 to 15 minutes. While still warm, roll in powdered sugar. After cooling, roll again in powdered sugar. Approximate yield: 9 dozen cookies.

Ann Mills
Queen Annes County Unit (Grasonville)

GLAZED FRESH APPLE COOKIES

½ cup shortening
1⅓ cups dark brown sugar,
  firmly packed
½ teaspoon salt
1 teaspoon cloves
1 teaspoon cinnamon
½ teaspoon nutmeg
1 egg, unbeaten

2 cups sifted flour
1 teaspoon soda
1 cup finely chopped,
  unpared apples
1 cup raisins
1 cup nuts
¼ cup apple juice or milk

Preheat oven to 400 degrees. Beat first 7 ingredients until smooth. Sift flour with soda; add ½ of flour to shortening mixture and blend; stir in fruit, nuts, raisins and liquid. Add remaining flour and mix well. Take up heaping teaspoonsful and push off onto greased cookie sheet with spatula. Bake for 11 to 14 minutes. Remove while still hot. Spread with a thin coating of vanilla glaze. Yield: 3½ dozen.

Mrs. Carole Anne Hickman
Kent County Unit (Millington)

CHERRY WINKS

¾ cup shortening
1 cup sugar
2 eggs
2 tablespoons milk
1 teaspoon vanilla
2¼ cups flour
1 teaspoon baking
  powder

½ teaspoon salt
½ teaspoon soda
1 cup chopped pecans
1 cup chopped dates
⅓ cup cherries
2½ cups crushed corn
  flakes

Preheat oven to 375 degrees. Cream shortening and sugar together; add 2 eggs, milk and vanilla; mix well. Sift dry ingredients together and gradually mix into the creamed mixture. Add pecans, dates and cherries. Drop by the teaspoonful into corn flakes; toss lightly to coat them; then form into balls and place ¼ of a cherry on each ball. Bake for 12 to 15 minutes. Yield: 5 dozen.

Pauline B. Callahan
Talbot County Unit (Easton)

"CRY BABIES" COOKIES

1 cup butter or margarine
1 cup sugar
1 cup black molasses
5 cups flour
2 teaspoon cinnamon
2 teaspoons ginger

1 teaspoon nutmeg
1/4 teaspoon salt
1 tablespoon baking soda
1 cup boiling water
1 egg

Preheat oven to 375 degrees. Cream butter, sugar and molasses in a large mixing bowl. Sift flour with cinnamon, ginger, nutmeg, salt and soda, and add to mixture, combining thoroughly. Add boiling water and mix well. Finally, break egg into mixture and stir well. Drop by teaspoon, 2 inches apart, onto greased cookie sheet. Bake for 10 to 12 minutes or until surface of cookie leaves no indentation when lightly touched. *Do not overcook.* Yield: about 5 dozen cookies.

Note: Test sample baking. In some ovens, it may be wise to bake cookies for 5 to 6 minutes on bottom shelf and finish baking for 5 to 6 minutes on top shelf of oven. If cookies appear dry after storage, place in plastic bag with 1/4 of an apple to restore moisture.

Louisa M. Wallis
Cecil County Unit (North East)

TOP OF THE STOVE COOKIES

1/2 cup butter
3/4 cup sugar
1/2 cup chopped dates
2 egg yolks

1 teaspoon vanilla
2 cups Rice Crispies
1/2 cup chopped nuts
Powdered sugar

Melt butter; add sugar, dates and egg yolks. Cook 10 minutes in a heavy pan on top of the stove (don't overcook). Add vanilla. Pour over Rice Crispies and nuts. Roll into balls and dip in powdered sugar.

Elvira F. Merrill
Mid Anne Arundel Unit (Crofton)

SCHAEFER'S WAFERS

2 egg whites, room temperature	1/2 teaspoon vanilla
2/3 cup sugar	1 (6-ounce) package chocolate chips

Preheat oven to 375 degrees. Beat egg whites until stiff; gradually add sugar and beat for about 5 minutes. Add vanilla and gently fold in chocolate chips. Drop by teaspoonful onto an ungreased cookie sheet. Place in oven and count to 10. Turn oven off and leave overnight or for 6 hours. Yield: 4 dozen.

William D. Schaefer, Mayor
City of Baltimore

DATE RUM BALLS

2 eggs	1 cup coconut
1 cup sugar	1 teaspoon vanilla
1 cup chopped dates	2 teaspoons rum extract
1 cup chopped nuts	

Preheat oven to 300 degrees. Beat eggs well. Add sugar and beat. Blend in remaining ingredients. Turn into a 2-quart casserole. Bake for 30 minutes. Remove from oven and while hot, beat with a wooden spoon. Cool until ready to handle. Form into small balls. Roll in granulated sugar. Yield: 3 to 4 dozen cookies.

Mabel I. Pruitt
Worcester County Unit (Snow Hill)

PEANUT BUTTER COOKIES

1/2 cup peanut butter	1 egg
1/2 cup shortening	1 1/2 cups flour
1/2 cup sugar	1/2 teaspoon baking soda
1/2 cup brown sugar	1/2 teaspoon salt

Preheat oven to 350 degrees. Cream all ingredients together. Roll into 1-inch balls; place on ungreased cookie sheet; press crisscross design into each cookie using fork prongs. Bake for 8 to 10 minutes. Makes 3 dozen.

Joanne Stephens
Northern Charles County Unit (Waldorf)

PEANUT COOKIES

1 1/2 cups shortening
1 cup white sugar
1 cup brown sugar
2 eggs
2 cups all-purpose flour,
  sifted
1 teaspoon soda

1 teaspoon baking
  powder
1 teaspoon salt
2 cups oatmeal
1 cup uncrushed corn
  flakes
1 cup salted peanuts

Preheat oven to 400 degrees. Cream shortening and gradually add sugars. Add 2 eggs; stir well. Mix dry ingredients and stir a small amount into shortening mixture. Stir well after each addition of dry ingredients until they all have been used. Stir in oatmeal, 1 cup at a time, and mix well. Stir in 1 cup corn flakes very slowly. *Do not crush* peanuts, use whole and fold into batter. Drop onto lightly greased cookie sheet. Bake for 10 minutes or until done. Cool. Yield: 48 average sized cookies.

JoAnn Clower
Oxon Hill/Clinton Unit

APPLE SQUARES

2 cups whole wheat flour
1/4 cup toasted wheat germ
2 teaspoons baking soda
1 teaspoon salt
1 teaspoon cinnamon
1/2 teaspoon nutmeg
4 cups diced, peeled tart
  apples

1 cup sugar
1 cup brown sugar
1 cup Wesson oil
1 cup walnuts
2 eggs
1 teaspoon vanilla

Preheat oven to 350 degrees. Stir together flour, wheat germ, baking soda, cinnamon, salt and nutmeg; set aside. In large bowl combine apples, brown sugar, white sugar, oil, walnuts, eggs and vanilla. Add flour mixture, blend well. Turn into greased 13-x-9-x-2 inch pan. Bake for 50 minutes. Cool and cut into squares.

Mrs. Mary Lee Johnson
Bel Air Unit (Bel Air)

AMAZING CHOCOLATE BROWNIES

1 cup white granulated
  sugar
½ cup margarine
1 (16-ounce) can
  Hershey's
  chocolate syrup

4 eggs
1 cup flour
1 cup chopped nuts,
  (optional)

Preheat oven to 350 degrees. Combine margarine and sugar; add chocolate syrup and eggs, one at a time. Add flour and nuts. Pour in 14-x-11-inch sheet cake pan. (Can also use jelly roll pan.) Bake for 25 minutes in sheet cake pan; 20 minutes if using jelly roll pan.

Icing:

½ cup margarine
1½ cups white granulated
  sugar

⅓ cup evaporated milk
½ cup chocolate chips

Bring margarine, sugar and milk to boil for 1 minute; add chocolate chips. Pour immediately onto warm brownies.
Note: Quick and easy! Always super moist and delicious!

Carol A. Kirchner
Allegany County Unit (Cumberland)

BROWN SUGAR BROWNIES

⅔ cup butter or margarine
1 pound brown sugar
3 eggs
2¾ cups cake flour
2 teaspoons baking
  powder

¼ teaspoon salt
1 teaspoon almond
  extract
1 package butterscotch
  bits

Preheat oven to 350 degrees. Melt butter and sugar, slowly, so as not to burn. Cool. Add eggs, one at a time, beating briefly after each addition. Sift dry ingredients and add almond extract and butterscotch bits. Bake at 350 degrees for 20 minutes in a 12-x-9-inch baking pan. Test with toothpick for doneness. Allow 10 minutes more if a well-done brownie is preferred.

Phyllis R. Miller
Metro Centre Unit (Baltimore)

PECAN PIE

3 eggs
1 cup dark corn syrup
2 tablespoons melted
   butter
1 tablespoon vanilla

1 cup sugar
1 tablespoon flour
¹/₂ teaspoon salt
1 cup pecans
1 unbaked pie shell

Preheat oven to 350 degrees. Beat eggs until just mixed. Add corn syrup, melted butter and vanilla. Mix sugar, flour, salt and add to egg mixture. Place pecans on bottom of unbaked pie shell, then pour in the mixture. Bake 1 hour.

Harriett M. Reichard
Talbot County (Easton)

Similar recipes submitted by:
Sherry Noren
Caroline County Unit (Denton)
Paula Wolpe
Montgomery County Unit (Chevy Chase)
Mary Lou Clem
Northern Charles County Unit (Oxon Hill)

SWEET POTATO PIE

3 large sweet potatoes
1 cup butter
5 large eggs
2 cups sugar
1 cup milk

1 tablespoon vanilla
   extract
1 tablespoon lemon
   extract

Preheat oven to 300 degrees. Boil sweet potatoes for 20 minutes or longer, if necessary. When potatoes are done, place them in a large mixing bowl; add butter, sugar, and eggs; beat slowly to eliminate strings from potatoes. Add milk and extracts. Stir until mixture is firm and pour into 3 (9-inch) pastry shells. Bake for 30 minutes. Yield: three 9-inch pies or 2 deep-dish pies.

Sylvia Scott Butler
Lower Park Heights/Forest Park Unit (Baltimore)

STRAWBERRY WHIP

1 cup strawberries, sliced   1 egg white
1 cup sugar

Whip egg white and sugar until it stands in stiff peaks. Fold in strawberries. Serve over pound cake slices or dessert cups.

Doris W. Tettimer
Calvert County Unit (St. Leonard)

APPLE PIE

1 package pie crust mix
10 cooking apples, peeled
   and sliced
²/₃ cup sugar
1 teaspoon ground
   cinnamon

¹/₄ teaspoon nutmeg
¹/₈ to ¹/₄ cup milk
2 teaspoons butter

Preheat oven to 350 degrees. Make pie crust as directed on package. Cover pie pan with 1 layer of crust. Place apple slices in pie pan until filled. Sprinkle sugar and cinnamon over apples until covered with a thin layer. Sprinkle nutmeg over cinnamon. Cover with second pie crust. Seal edges. Using a pastry brush, brush milk over entire crust. Place ¹/₂ teaspoon pieces of butter around center of crust. Make 3 to 4 slits in top of pie crust. Bake for 35 to 40 minutes or until crust is golden brown.
Note: Try topping with ice cream. It fills the house with a wonderful aroma and it tastes delicious!

Susan Markus
Northwest Community Unit (Baltimore)

Variation: Add ¹/₂ cup chopped nuts.

Jill L. Smith
Kent County Unit (Chestertown)

SAWADA'S PEACH PIE

3¹/₂-4 quarts sliced fresh
  peaches
¹/₂ pint heavy cream
1¹/₂ cups sugar
3 to 4 tablespoons
  cornstarch

2 to 3 teaspoons vanilla
2 packages Pet Milk or
  A & P Brand deep dish
  pie crusts

Preheat oven to 500 degrees. Layer peaches in pie shells. Mix cream, sugar, vanilla and cornstarch in a small bowl. Pour over peaches. Cover with lattice or whole top crust. Bake at 500 degrees (important temperature) for 30 minutes; reduce heat to 325 degrees and continue baking until golden brown.
Note: A family recipe from Allegany County for 50-60 years.

Edward A. Sawada, M.D.
Division of Cancer Control, Department of Health & Mental Hygiene
Towson County Unit

CHOCOLATE MOUSSE PIE

2 (1.5-ounce) envelopes
  whipped topping mix
1¹/₂ cups milk
2 (4¹/₂-ounce) packages
  chocolate instant
  pudding mix
¹/₄ cup DeKuyper
  Amaretto liqueur

1 (9-inch) pastry shell,
  baked and cooled
1 pint whipping cream
2 teaspoons sugar
1 teaspoon vanilla

Prepare topping mix according to package directions. Add milk, pudding mix, and Amaretto; beat 2 minutes at high speed of an electric mixer. Spoon mixture into pastry shell. Beat whipping cream at high speed of electric mixer until cream forms soft peaks. Add sugar and vanilla and beat 30 seconds longer. Top pie with whipped cream. Chill at least 4 hours. Yield: 8 servings.
Note: Pie can be made 2 days in advance if whipped cream is not put on until served. Cover with plastic wrap and keep refrigerated.

Marlene Blankley
Western Charles County Unit (Indian Head)

RHUBARB PIE

1 (9-inch) pastry shell
2 to 3 cups rhubarb, cut in
  ¹/₂-inch pieces
1 cup sugar
3 eggs, separated
2 tablespoons flour

Bake the pastry shell for about 5 minutes at 350 degrees. Cool. Arrange cubed rhubarb in the bottom of the shell. Mix the sugar, egg yolks, and flour. Drop the mixture over the rhubarb and dot generously with butter. Bake at 350 degrees for 30 minutes or until the rhubarb is soft. Use the egg whites to make your favorite meringue recipe. Spread meringue over pie and bake at 350 degrees until golden brown. For those who like rhubarb, you will love this pie.

Harriet M. Allen
Bel Air Unit (Churchville)

PEANUT BUTTER CHEESE PIE

Filling:
3 (3-ounce) packages
  cream cheese
¹/₂ cup peanut butter
  (creamy or chunky)
2 eggs
¹/₂ cup sugar
1 teaspoon vanilla
¹/₄ teaspoon cinnamon
1 (9-inch) graham cracker
  crust

Preheat oven to 350 degrees. Blend above ingredients in blender on slow *or* use hand mixer on medium speed until blended together. Fill crust and bake for 30 minutes.

Topping:
2 cups sour cream
¹/₄ teaspoon vanilla
¹/₈ teaspoon cinnamon
1 small container
  Cool Whip

Mix all ingredients together using hand mixer on slow speed. If too tart, add 1 teaspoon powdered sugar. Spoon on top of pie and chill overnight. Pie is best if chilled overnight, but can be served before then if set. Yield: 6 to 8 servings.

Lisa Seldomridge
Wicomico County Unit (Parsonsburg)

LIQUEUR PIE

Crust:

1 cup graham cracker or
  chocolate wafer crumbs
¹/₄ cup melted butter
  or margarine

¹/₄ cup sifted powdered
  sugar (if using graham
  crackers only)

Preheat oven to 300 degrees. Crush crumbs or put in blender until very fine. Stir in sugar and butter until well blended. Press into a 9-inch pie pan. Bake for 15 minutes.

Filling:

¹/₂ cup cold water
1 envelope Knox gelatin
²/₃ cup sugar
3 eggs, separated
¹/₄ cup each of 2 liqueurs
  of your choice (such as
  Amoretto, Tia Maria or
  Drambuie or you may
  substitute ¹/₄ cup
  brandy for 1 liqueur)

1 cup whipping cream
¹/₂ teaspoon cream of
  tartar

Put water, gelatin and sugar into a saucepan with beaten egg yolks. Heat until dissolved and thickened, but do not boil. Add liqueurs and cool until it starts to mound. Whip cream; whip egg whites with cream of tartar. Mix cream and egg whites into gelatin mixture. Pour into crust and chill. Can be prepared a day before use.

Pearl Weisfield
Montgomery County Unit (Rockville)

STRAWBERRY PIE

1 quart fresh strawberries	½ cup water
1 cup sugar	1 tablespoon butter
3 tablespoons cornstarch	1 (9-inch) baked pastry shell

Mash enough strawberries to make 1 cup of pulp (about 1 pint). Combine sugar and cornstarch; mix well. Add water and pulp. Cook stirring constantly, until thick and translucent (about 10 minutes). Stir in butter and cool. Place remaining uncooked strawberries in bottom of cooled pastry shell. Cover with cooked mixture. Place in refrigerator for 2 hours. Serve with whipped cream.

Juanita R. Cochrane
Talbot County Unit (St. Michaels)

ALMOND RUM CREAM PIE

⅔ cup finely granulated sugar	1 (9-inch) graham cracker crust, chilled
⅓ cup cake flour	½ cup almonds, blanched and toasted
Generous dash of salt	
2 large eggs, slightly beaten	1 cup whipping cream, whipped
½ cup rum, divided	¼ cup graham cracker crumbs
1½ cups scalded milk	

Sift sugar, flour and salt into top of a double boiler. Stir in eggs with 3 tablespoons rum. When thoroughly blended, stir in scalded milk with 5 tablespoons rum, very gradually, almost drop by drop. Cook over hot water, stirring constantly, until the mixture thickens. *Cool.* Sprinkle crust with almonds and pour in rum cream filling. Cover with whipped cream and garnish with graham cracker crumbs.
Note: Pie may be garnished with shaved chocolate instead of the graham cracker crumbs.

Mrs. Minnie L. Godfrey
Dorchester County Unit (Cambridge)

APPLE CRISP CRUSTLESS SPOON PIE

2 pounds eating apples
1 (6-ounce) can undiluted,
  thawed unsweetened
  apple juice concentrate
2 tablespoons cornstarch
6 tablespoons raisins

1½ teaspoons cinnamon,
  divided
6 tablespoons Grape-Nuts
  or other crushed
  breakfast cereal

Preheat oven to 375 degrees. Peel and slice apples thinly. Mix with apple juice, cornstarch, raisins and 1 teaspoon cinnamon. Spoon into an 8 or 9-inch nonstick pie pan. Stir cereal with remaining ½ teaspoon cinnamon and sprinkle over fruit. Bake uncovered for 25 to 30 minutes, until apples are soft and topping is browned. Spoon into dessert cups and serve warm. Makes 8 servings.

Mrs. Margaret B. Palmer
Carroll County Unit (Finksburg)

APPLE PAN DOWDY

Sliced Apples
Cinnamon
1 cup flour
1½ cups sugar
1 teaspoon baking
  powder

¾ teaspoon salt
1 egg, slightly beaten
⅓ cup melted butter

Preheat oven to 350 degrees. Butter a 9-x-9-inch pan. Place apples in pan as for a pie. Sprinkle generously with cinnamon. Sift together flour, sugar, baking powder, and salt. Add egg and melted butter. Mix and spread over apples (not too thick in middle as it takes too long to bake). Bake about 40 minutes or until dough is done when tested with toothpick in middle.

Helen Stetson
Montgomery County Unit (Silver Spring)

QUICK COBBLER

¹/₂ cup butter or margarine	³/₄ cup milk
1 cup sugar	1 (1-pound) can pie filling
1 cup flour	
1 tablespoon baking powder	

Preheat oven to 375 degrees. Melt butter or margarine in an 8-inch square pan. Mix sugar, flour and baking powder. Combine dry ingredients with milk. Pour batter into pan of melted butter. Pour pie filling over the dough. Bake for 45 minutes.

Linda Hill
Southern Charles County Unit (Waldorf)

WHITE POTATO PIE

6 to 8 medium potatoes	1 large can evaporated milk
¹/₂ cup butter	
2 cups sugar	1¹/₂ teaspoons lemon or vanilla extract
4 eggs, beaten	

Preheat oven to 350 degrees. Cook and mash potatoes, add remaining ingredients and mix well. Pour into pastry shell, sprinkle top with nutmeg and bake for about 1 hour or until custard is firm.

Madlyn E. Wooters
Queen Annes County Unit (Queenstown)

CANDY CRISPIES

1 cup dark corn syrup	5 cups Rice Krispies
1 cup sugar	1 cup coconut
1 cup half and half	1 cup salted peanuts
6 cups cornflakes	

Boil syrup, sugar and cream together until it reaches the firm ball stage. Combine cereals, coconut and nuts in a large bowl. Pour syrup over and mix thoroughly. Press into a 13-x-9-x-2 inch buttered pan. Cut into squares when cool. Yield: 1¹/₂ to 2 dozen.

Mrs. Edmund W. Rupert
Merle/Duval Unit (Lanham)

SIN (CHOCOLATE OR LEMON)

1 cup flour
1/2 cup softened margarine
1 cup nuts (1/2 cup finely
  chopped)
1 cup powdered sugar
1 (8-ounce) package
  softened cream cheese
12 ounces Cool Whip,
  partially defrosted

1 teaspoon vanilla
  extract
1 large or 2 small boxes
  instant pudding mix
  (chocolate or lemon)
3 1/2 cups milk

1st layer: Mix flour, margarine and 1/2 cup nuts. Press into 13-x-9-x-2-inch pan (covering will be thin). Bake 25 minutes at 350 degrees. Cool.

2nd layer: Cream powdered sugar, cream cheese and 6 ounces Cool Whip and 1 teaspoon vanilla. Mix thoroughly. Gently spread over baked crust.

3rd layer: Prepare instant pudding according to directions *for pie*. Pour over 2nd layer and chill until firm (about 5 to 10 minutes).

4th layer: Top with remaining 6 ounces Cool Whip and sprinkle with nuts. Chill several hours before serving. May also be frozen for a few days.

Mrs. Florence Siebert
Montgomery County Unit (Silver Spring)

BLUEBERRY DESSERT

1/2 pound vanilla wafers,
  crushed
1 cup powdered sugar
1/2 cup margarine
2 eggs

1 can blueberry pie filling
1 cup whipping cream (or
1 package Dream Whip)
1/2 cup nuts

Spread half of wafer crumbs in bottom of a 9-inch square glass pan. Cream margarine and sugar. Add eggs one at a time. Beat well. Spread over crumbs. Spread blueberry pie filling over egg mixture. Spread whipped cream on top. Sprinkle on nuts then remaining crumbs. Refrigerate 24 hours.

Joyce Keavenly
St. Marys County Unit (Hollywood)

GRAHAM CRACKER PRALINES

1 cup brown sugar,
  firmly packed
1 cup butter
1 cup chopped pecans

Graham crackers
(enough to cover a
cookie sheet)

Preheat oven to 350 degrees. Combine sugar and butter in a saucepan; bring to a boil; boil for 2 minutes. Remove from heat and stir in chopped pecans. Pour over graham crackers, which have been placed close together on a cookie sheet. (Crackers should be close enough to form a solid sheet.) Spread mixture evenly over graham crackers. Bake for 10 minutes. Cool slightly and cut into squares.

Mrs. Jean A. Bibby
Allegany County Unit (Cumberland)

CRÈME BRÛLÉE

4 cups heavy cream
2 tablespoons sugar
7 egg yolks

2 teaspoons vanilla
1/2 cup light brown
  sugar

Heat cream in top of double boiler until steam begins to rise. Add sugar and stir until dissolved. Beat egg yolks until light colored and add slowly to cream. Add vanilla. Mix well and pour into a 13-x-9-x-2 inch glass baking dish. (Custard should be about 1 1/2 inches deep.) Place dish in pan of hot water and bake at 325 degrees until custard is set (about 15 minutes). Cool and chill thoroughly for 3 to 4 hours in refrigerator. Sift 1/4 inch brown sugar over top of custard. Place under pre-heated broiler in a very hot oven and watch carefully until sugar melts and runs together, leaving a shiny caramel topping. Cool and chill again at least 2 hours before serving. Serves 12.

Mrs. Patricia Hughes
Wife of Governor Harry Hughes
State of Maryland
Note: Mrs. Hughes founded the First Ladies Brigade in 1980 to encourage special events in Maryland Division. She has been an active volunteer for the American Cancer Society throughout the entire state.

CHOCOLATE TORTE

Crust:

1⅓ cups crushed graham crackers

3 tablespoons sugar

3 tablespoons unsweetened cocoa

⅓ cup melted butter

Blend crackers, sugar, cocoa and melted butter. Press onto bottom and sides of a spring form pan. Bake at 350 degrees for 10 minutes. Cool.

Filling:

4 (3-ounce) packages cream cheese

¾ cup sugar

2 eggs

1 tablespoon coffee liqueur or rum

1 teaspoon vanilla

8 ounces sour cream

1 square grated unsweetened chocolate

Beat cream cheese with electric mixer until fluffy. Beat in sugar gradually. Beat in eggs 1 at a time. Add liqueur and vanilla. Turn into baked crust. Bake at 350 degrees for 30 minutes. Cool 10 minutes on a wire rack. Gently spread sour cream over baked layer. Sprinkle with grated chocolate.

Topping:

1½ teaspoons instant coffee

2 tablespoons boiling water

4 squares semi-sweet chocolate

4 eggs, separated

⅓ cup sugar

1 tablespoon coffee liqueur or rum

½ teaspoon vanilla

½ cup heavy cream

Dissolve coffee in boiling water in double boiler. Add 4 squares chocolate. Stir until melted and blended. Beat 4 egg yolks until thick. Gradually beat sugar into the egg yolks. Add coffee-chocolate mixture gradually to the yolks. Add liqueur and vanilla. Beat egg whites until stiff and gently fold into chocolate. Spread over cooled layer. Refrigerate until firm (2 to 4 hours). Decorate with whipped cream.

Norma Parker
Frederick County Unit (Ijamsville)

SNOW CREAM

2 eggs, beaten
1/2 to 3/4 cup sugar
1 1/2 cups milk and/or cream

1 teaspoon vanilla
1 large bowl of new
fallen snow

Mix together the eggs, sugar, milk and vanilla. Beat until fluffy. Add enough snow to thicken.

Note: When I was a little girl, my mother made Snow Cream as often as we had snow. I found this recipe in a newspaper several years ago and it is delicious.

Diana Kaeding
Mid Anne Arundel Unit (Crofton)

BROEKEL TORTE

3 eggs
1 cup sugar
1 cup flour
1 teaspoon baking
   powder

1 pound chopped dates
1 cup chopped walnuts
Crushed pineapple
Whipped cream

Preheat oven to 325 degrees. Mix all ingredients, except pineapple and whipped cream; bake for 40 minutes in a 13-x-9-x-2-inch pan. Crumble after the cake has cooled. Place half of the crumbs on a serving plate and cover with crushed pineapple and whipped cream. Repeat the layers. Chill overnight to set. The sugar may be omitted without detriment to the results.

Carl W. Sadoti
South Potomac County Unit (Temple Hill)

COFFEE MARSHMALLOW DESSERT

15 large marshmallows
1/2 cup cooked coffee

1/2 tablespoon cocoa
1 cup whipping cream

Place marshmallows, coffee, and cocoa in top of double boiler. Cook until dissolved; *cool.* Whip cream until stiff. Add to *cooled* mixture; blend thoroughly. Chill. Serves 4.

Mrs. Roger M. Kelly
Talbot County Unit (Oxford)

CHOCOLATE ALMOND FROZEN MOUSSE

Crust:

1 cup all-purpose flour
1/2 cup firmly packed
   brown sugar

1/2 cup ground almonds
1/2 cup butter or
   margarine, melted

Preheat oven to 350 degrees. Combine all crust ingredients; mix until crumbly. Spread in a 13-x-9-x-2-inch pan. Bake at 350 degrees for 10 to 15 minutes or until light golden brown, stirring once; cool. Spread 2 cups crumbs in bottom of ungreased 9 or 10-inch springform pan (reserve remaining crumbs for topping).

Filling:

4 eggs, separated
1/4 cup milk
1 teaspoon almond
   extract

1 can ready to spread
   chocolate fudge frosting
1 cup whipping cream,
   whipped

In small saucepan, beat egg yolks slightly; add milk. Cook over medium heat, stirring constantly, until thick. Remove from heat; stir in almond extract. In large bowl, fold egg yolk mixture into frosting. In another large bowl, beat egg whites until stiff peaks form. Fold both egg whites and whipped cream into frosting; pour over prepared crumbs. Freeze 1 hour; sprinkle with reserved crumbs. Freeze 4 hours or until firm. If desired, serve with additional whipped cream. Yield: 12 servings.

Angie Como Linn
Laurel/Beltsville Unit (Laurel)

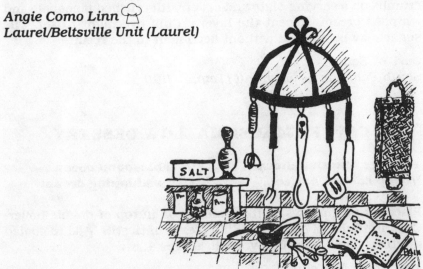

MINIATURE CHEESE CUPS

1 pound cream cheese
¾ cup sugar

3 eggs
1 teaspoon vanilla

Preheat oven to 375 degrees. Cream together well the cream cheese and sugar. Add 1 egg at a time beating well after each. Add vanilla. Pour into very small paper cupcake containers (placed on trays or muffin pans). Bake for 15 minutes. When this is done, remove from oven and put 1 teaspoon of second mixture on each one and place trays back in oven for 5 minutes.

Second mixture:

¼ cup sugar
1 teaspoon vanilla

½ pint sour cream

Mix together and put 1 teaspoon on each cheese cup. Allow to cool at least 15 to 30 minutes and top with a prepared pie filling (cherries or blueberries). Makes 36.

Sue Ann Tabler
Carroll County Unit (Sykesville)

ANGEL FOOD DELIGHT

2 envelopes Knox gelatin
¼ cup cold water
1 cup boiling water
1 cup sugar
1 (20-ounce) can crushed
   pineapple, undrained
Juice of 1 lemon

4 packages Dream Whip
1 large angel food cake
   (can be bought)
1 (3-ounce) can flaked
   coconut
8 to 10 maraschino cherries

In large mixing bowl, dissolve 2 envelopes gelatin in cold water. Add boiling water, sugar and stir until dissolved. Add crushed pineapple and lemon juice. Refrigerate until it starts to congeal. Whip 2 packages Dream Whip according to package directions and fold into gelatin mixture. Break cake into chunks and fold into mixture. Chill for approximately 24 hours. Unmold and frost with the other 2 packages of Dream Whip. Decorate with coconut and cherries. May use a large tube pan or spring form pan, which has been lightly sprayed with non-stick cooking spray.

Mrs. Shirley C. Fradin
Northwest Community Unit (Baltimore)

ORANGE PUDDING

3 oranges, peeled and cut
in small pieces
1/2 cup sugar
2 eggs, separated

3 tablespoons sugar
1 tablespoon cornstarch
1/4 cup milk
1 pint milk

Place cut up orange pieces in a 1 1/2 quart baking dish. Pour sugar over orange pieces and let set until sugar dissolves. Combine 2 egg yolks, 3 tablespoons sugar, cornstarch and 1/4 cup milk. Pour custard into 1 pint milk which has been brought to a boil; stir until mixture thickens. Let cool and pour over oranges. Use the whites of the 2 eggs and beat until stiff (1 teaspoon sugar can be added if desired). Cover the custard with meringue and brown in oven.
Note: If you wish to omit the meringue, whole eggs can be put in the custard mixture.

Ruth E. Myers
Carroll County Unit (Taneytown)

LEMON BREAD PUDDING

3 cups skim milk
4 slices bread, cubed
3 eggs, well beaten
4 1/2 teaspoons artificial
sweetener

Rind of lemon
2 tablespoons lemon juice
1/4 teaspoon almond
extract

Preheat oven to 350 degrees. Pour milk over bread cubes; let stand 10 minutes. Combine remaining ingredients and blend well. Stir lightly into bread cubes. Pour into a greased 1 1/2 quart casserole. Set in a pan of hot water. Bake at 350 degrees for 45 to 60 minutes, or until golden brown and custard is set. Makes 6 servings.
Note: Each serving contains 126 calories; if made with sugar. each serving would contain 222 calories.

Edna W. Govan
Oxon Hill/Clinton Unit (Oxon Hill)

Jarrett Manor

Selman Wright

VINEGAR TARTS

1 cup butter
1 1/2 cups sugar
4 to 6 tablespoons vinegar
2 eggs, beaten
2 teaspoons flour

2 (9-inch) pastry shells or
pastry to make
approximately 48 small
tarts using tassie pans

Preheat oven to 350 degrees. Cream butter and sugar; add eggs, vinegar and flour. Pour filling into pastry and bake for 30 minutes if using pastry shells, or approximately 15 minutes for tarts.

Mrs. Betty Ann Grant
Kent County Unit (Chestertown)

SPICED BREAD PUDDING

2 cups dry bread cubes
4 cups milk, scalded
¾ cup sugar
1 tablespoon butter
¼ teaspoon salt
⅛ teaspoon nutmeg

½ teaspoon cinnamon
¼ teaspoon ginger
4 eggs, slightly beaten
2 teaspoons vanilla
   extract
¼ cup raisins

Preheat oven to 350 degrees. Soak bread in milk 5 minutes. Add sugar, butter, salt and spices. Pour slowly over eggs. Add vanilla and raisins; mix well. Pour into buttered 1½-quart casserole or baking dish. Bake in pan of hot water for 1 hour or until silver knife comes out clean when inserted in center. Makes 8 to 10 servings.

Barbara Tiller
First District Harford Unit (Abingdon)

RICE PUDDING

2 cups milk
2 eggs, slightly beaten
½ cup sugar
1 cup cooked rice, (not
   instant)

1 teaspoon vanilla
   extract
Nutmeg, cinnamon or
   sugar to sprinkle on top

Preheat oven to 350 degrees. Bring milk to boil; then add eggs, sugar, rice, and vanilla. Pour into greased loaf pan or small casserole dish. Sprinkle with nutmeg, cinnamon or sugar. Place in pan of water and bake for 1 hour. Should be firm when done. *Note: Can add jelly, raisins, or marmalade if desired.*

Phyllis Weisberg
Northwest Community Unit (Baltimore)

Down Home Accompaniments

Riding to Hounds—Tara Moore
Hounds following the Hunt in Howard County. There is still a very active Howard County Hunt Club as pictured here by Tara Moore.

EASTERN SHORE HOMEMADE SCRAPPLE

2 hog heads or equal pounds pork scraps	Salt
Water	Pepper
½ small hog liver	Sage
1 or 2 hog hearts	Flour
1 or 2 hog tongues	Corn meal

Cook all ingredients until tender in salted water. When well-done, drain (reserving liquid), cool, and put through a food grinder. Combine ground meat and the liquid. Divide into two large cookers to give plenty of room for thickening and stirring. Add 6 tablespoons of pepper and 6 tablespoons of sage *to each cooker.* Adjust salt, pepper, and sage to suit your taste. Bring to a boil, stirring constantly. Add to this mixture a thickening made from half flour and half ground meal, mixed. Add enough meal and flour, stirring constantly, until a spoon will stand alone in the mixture. Press into 13-x-9-x-2 inch pans. Spoon off any grease from top as it accumulates. Keep refrigerated. May be frozen for 1 to 2 months.

Mrs. Sarah Blunt
Queen Annes County Unit (Centreville)

PICKLED PIGS FEET

8 pigs feet	3 teaspoons salt
2 or 3 large onions, quartered	2 teaspoons black pepper
	1 cup vinegar
4 stalks celery, cut up	4 to 6 quarts water

Wash and scrub pigs feet until clean. Place feet in three quarts of water and bring to a rolling boil. Add onions, celery, salt and pepper. Cook on medium flame adding water as necessary. After 2 hours add vinegar; continue cooking 1½ to 2 hours more, or until tender. Serve with potato salad. Yield: 8 servings.

William Washington, Jr.
Communities United Unit (Landover)

CANNED FRESH SAUSAGE

5 pounds fresh pork
  sausage
2 or 3 15-x-10-x-1 inch
  baking pans

6 pint jars with lids
  and rings

Preheat oven to 350 degrees. Make small sausage patties to fit pint jars after cooking. Place on baking pans. Cook in oven for 20 to 25 minutes. Place cooked sausage into a large iron skillet with grease. Brown over high heat, turning often to brown all sides. When browned, fill jars with sausage patties. Pour hot grease over sausage. Seal with lids and rings. Turn jars upside down so grease will remain on top of jar. Place on a towel and cover. Repeat until all sausage is in jars. This will keep as long as jars are sealed and kept upside down.
Note: To use: Put jars upside down in a saucepan of cold water. Turn on heat and when the grease in the top of the jar has melted remove sausage patties from the jar. Heat in an iron skillet until warm; drain on paper towels. Delicious with hot cakes or biscuits!

Mary A. Larrimore
Caroline County Unit (Ridgely)

CANNED SPAGHETTI SAUCE

½ bushel ripe tomatoes
1 tablespoon sweet basil
3 pounds onions, peeled
  and chopped
1 bud garlic, peeled and
  minced

8 (6-ounce) cans tomato
  paste
½ cup sugar
½ cup salt
1 pint oil

Blanch tomatoes in hot water and peel. Using a blender or food processor, mix onions, garlic and sweet basil. Gradually add tomato paste. Add sugar, salt, and oil and stir well. Cook, stirring occassionally, until it comes to a full boil. Simmer for 10 minutes. Pour into hot sterilized jars and seal. When opening for use, add 1 package of dry McCormick Spaghetti Sauce to each can.

Emily Byer
Allegany County Unit

CRANBERRY-ORANGE CHUTNEY

1 cup fresh orange
  sections
1/2 cup orange juice
4 cups fresh or frozen
  cranberries
2 cups sugar

1 cup apples, unpeeled
  and chopped
1/2 cup white raisins
1/4 cup walnuts, chopped
1/2 teaspoon ginger
1/2 teaspoon cinnamon

Combine all ingredients in a large saucepan and bring to a boil. Reduce heat and simmer for 5 minutes or until berries begin to burst. Remove from heat and stir occasionally while cooling. Refrigerate until serving time. Makes 5 1/2 cups.

Note: Keeps well-also makes nice Christmas gifts when put into a pretty jar.

Mary Lee Johnson
Bel Air Unit (Bel Air)

CLAIRE'S CRANBERRY PRESERVES

1 pound fresh cranberries
1 (6-ounce) can frozen
  orange or apple juice
  concentrate
1 tablespoon minute
  tapioca

2 oranges, 1 peeled, 1
  unpeeled
2 apples, unpeeled
3 tablespoons honey

Cook cranberries in undiluted juice concentrate for a few minutes. Remove from heat and add tapioca. Grind apples and oranges and add to cranberries. Add honey, using more if needed to suit your taste. Refrigerate overnight before using to blend flavors.

Marion D. Vosseler
Northeastern Baltimore County Unit (Perry Hall)

GLAZED CARROTS, RADISHES, AND PEAS

1/2 cup butter or
  margarine
1/4 cup water
1 tablespoon lemon juice
3 (6-ounce) packages
  radishes
3 (16-ounce) cans small
  whole carrots, drained

1 (20-ounce) bag frozen
  green peas
1 1/2 teaspoons salt
3/4 teaspoon sugar
1/2 teaspoon pepper

About 45 minutes before serving bring butter, water, lemon juice and radishes to a boil in a 6-quart saucepan. Reduce heat to low; cover; simmer for 30 minutes or until radishes are tender, stirring often. Add remaining ingredients; cook 10 minutes or until carrots and peas are heated through, stirring ocassionally. Serves 10.

Mrs. Edward Henning (Irene)
Southeastern Baltimore Unit (Baltimore)

CUCUMBER PICKLES

5 quarts cucumbers,
  unpeeled and sliced
8 onions, sliced

2 green peppers, sliced
1/2 cup salt

Place cucumbers, onions, and peppers into a large bowl; pour salt over and mix. Add two trays of ice cubes and cover with a weighted plate. Let stand for 3 to 4 hours.

Syrup:
5 cups white wine vinegar
5 cups sugar
1/2 teaspoon tumeric

1/2 teaspoon ground cloves
1 teaspoon celery seed
2 teaspoons mustard seed

Bring syrup ingredients to a boil in a large pan. Add the drained, washed cucumber mixture. Bring to a boil again, stirring frequently. As soon as it comes to a boil, remove from heat and pack into hot sterilized jars; seal.

Kathleen Gunther
Caroline County Unit

COPPER PENNY CARROTS

2 pounds carrots, sliced
1 small green pepper,
thinly sliced
1 medium onion, thinly
sliced
1 (10³/₄-ounce) can
condensed tomato soup
¹/₂ cup salad oil

1 cup sugar
³/₄ cup apple cider
vinegar
1 teaspoon prepared
mustard
1 teaspoon Worcestershire
sauce
Salt and pepper

Cook carrots in salted water until tender crisp; drain. Arrange a
layer of carrot, green pepper and onion in a plastic bowl with a
tight fitting lid. Combine remaining ingredients in a saucepan
and bring to a boil, stirring until thoroughly blended. Pour over
the carrot mixture, cover and refrigerate overnight. Keeps well.
Serves 8.

Dorrie Christie
South County Unit (Galesville)

BEET PICKLES

1 gallon fresh beets
2 cups water
2 cups cider vinegar

3 cups sugar
1 tablespoon mixed
pickling spices

Cook whole unpeeled beets in water to cover until tender; drain
and peel beets. Place whole beets into hot sterilized jars. Combine
remaining ingredients and bring to a boil. Pour syrup over beets;
seal. Yield: 8 pints.

Bernice R. Forthman
Dorchester County Unit (Cambridge)

MAPLE SYRUP

2 cups sugar
1 cup water

1 teaspoon maple flavoring
1 teaspoon vanilla

Bring sugar and water mixture to a boil. Cook 3 minutes; remove
from heat. When cooled slightly, add flavorings. Serve over pancakes or waffles.

Sheila Hearn
Northern Baltimore City Unit (Baltimore)

BREAD AND BUTTER PICKLES

6 cups cucumbers, thinly
   sliced
1 pound onions, peeled
   and sliced

1 large green pepper,
   seeded and sliced
1/4 cup salt

Mix above ingredients together in a large bowl.
Syrup:
2 cups brown sugar
1/2 teaspoon tumeric
1/4 teaspoon ground cloves
1 tablespoon mustard
   seed

1/2 teaspoon celery seed
2 cups cider vinegar

Using a separate bowl, mix above ingredients well; cover and let
stand 3 to 4 hours, refrigerated. Remove from refrigerator and
bring to a boil in a large saucepan. Boil 5 minutes. Drain
vegetables in a colander; rinse well. Add vegetables to hot syrup
and heat slowly, stirring occasionally. Pour into hot sterilized
pint jars with lids. Process 6 minutes in a boiling water bath.
Seal. Yield: 4 pints.

F. Greer Pooley, LPN
First District Harford Unit (Edgewood)

SWEET POTATO PICKLE

1 quart sweet potatoes,
   cooked and diced
1 quart lima beans,
   cooked
1 quart corn, cooked
1 quart onions, chopped
   and cooked
1 quart green pepper,
   diced and cooked

1 quart green tomatoes,
   chopped and cooked
1 quart vinegar
2 pounds sugar
2 tablespoons mustard
   seed
2 tablespoons celery
   seed
2 tablespoons tumeric

Place all ingredients in an 8 to 10 quart Dutch oven or heavy
saucepan and cook until desired thickness is reached. Pour into
hot sterilized jars and seal. Yield: 10 to 12 pints.

Mrs. Frank Patchett
Queen Annes County Unit

GREEN TOMATO PRESERVES
WITH RASPBERRY GELATIN

3 cups firm green
   tomatoes
3 cups sugar
1 (3-ounce) box raspberry
   flavored gelatin

Sterilized jars
Paraffin

Process green tomatoes in a blender; add sugar. Store in refrigerator overnight. Remove from refrigerator next day and bring to a boil; simmer for 15 minutes, stirring frequently. Remove from heat and add gelatin. Pour into hot sterilized jars; cover with thin layer of melted paraffin; seal. Keep stored in refrigerator.
Note: This recipe was published in the Daily Times of Salisbury. It is a very good recipe to use up extra garden tomatoes!

Peyton Zeigler
Wicomico County Unit (Owings)

YELLOW SQUASH PICKLES

Base:
10 cups yellow squash,
   thinly sliced
2 cups onions, thinly
   sliced

4 green peppers, chopped

Layer and salt lightly. Let set for 1 hour.

Syrup:
2 cups cider vinegar
2 to 3 cups sugar

2 teaspoons mustard seed
2 teaspoons celery seed

Bring above ingredients to a boil in a large saucepan. Add squash, onion, and peppers; bring to a boil, stirring with a wooden spoon. Pour into hot sterilized jars and seal. Process jars in hot water bath for 10 minutes. Yield: 5 pints.
Note: For a double batch use 10 pounds squash and double liquid ingredients. Yield: 10 pints.

Gerry Spore
Calvert County Unit (Owings)

SWEET PICKLES

12 pounds fresh
  cucumbers
1 fresh egg
Salt for brine
11 teaspoons alum

1 gallon vinegar
8 pounds sugar
1 (1½-ounce) can pickling
  spices
1 (2-ounce) can tumeric

Place cucumbers in salt water to cover. The water should be salty enough to float a fresh egg. Take the egg out of the water before putting in cucumbers. Let stand one week. Remove cucumbers from brine, wash and place in clean water to cover. Let stand 24 hours. Mix alum with water to cover cucumbers. Place them in alum water; soak 6 hours. Drain off water. Slice cucumbers. Heat one gallon vinegar and pour over cucumber slices. Let stand 24 hours. Drain off vinegar. Using 8 pounds sugar to 12 pounds cucumbers, put in a layer of cucumbers, then a layer of sugar. Put pickling spice over sugar, sprinkle with a little tumeric. Repeat layers until all cucumbers and sugar are used. Let stand for 3 days. Pack in sterilized jars. Pour the sweet pickle juice over cucumber slices and seal.

Annie Taylor
Worcester County Unit (Snow Hill)
Similar recipe submitted by Hannah R. Henry
Caroline County Unit (Ridgely)

ZUCCHINI PICKLES

2 pounds small zucchini
2 medium onions
1/4 cup salt
2 cups white vinegar
1 cup sugar

1 teaspoon celery seed
1 teaspoon mustard seed
1 teaspoon tumeric
1/2 teaspoon powdered
  mustard

Wash zucchini. Cut unpeeled zucchini and peeled onions into very thin slices and drop into a crock or bowl. Cover with water and add salt. Let stand for 1 hour; drain. Mix remaining ingredients in a saucepan and bring to a boil. Pour over zucchini and onion. Let stand 1 hour. Place in a large kettle and bring to a boil. Cook for 3 minutes. pack into hot sterilized jars and seal. Yield: 3 pints.

Rose M. Hamilton
Dorchester County Unit (Cambridge)

JALAPÉNO RELISH

1 quart cherry tomatoes
1 medium green pepper,
  chopped
1 medium onion, chopped
2 medium fresh jalapéno
  pepper or hot red
  peppers

1 to 2 cloves garlic
1/2 cup vinegar
1 teaspoon salt
1 teaspoon sugar
Dash oregano
Dash cayenne
Dash cumin

In blender container, food processor, or food grinder, coarsely grind unpeeled tomatoes; add green pepper, onion, jalapénos, and garlic to tomatoes; process until vegetables are coarsely ground. Stir in vinegar, salt and sugar. Transfer vegetables to a 3-quart saucepan. Simmer, uncovered, over low heat about 25 minutes or until desired consistency is reached. Stir in oregano, cayenne, and cumin; season to taste with salt. Store in refrigerator in a tightly covered container. Yield: 2 1/4 cups.
Note: May also be processed in a boiling water bath for 5 to 10 minutes in pint or half-pint jars.

Elaine W. Tracy
Mid Anne Arundel Unit (Millersville)

BRANDIED PEACHES

1 bushel firm ripe peaches   1 pint brandy
10 pounds sugar   6 quart jars

Peel peaches and fill jars. Pour in sugar until all spaces are filled; add ¼ cup brandy to each jar. Close jars; turn upside down overnight and tighten the lids the next day. Wrap all jars with newspaper and rags and store in a dark place. If possible, dig a deep hole in the ground, line with pine needles and rags, bury jars and cover with dirt until Christmas. This goes well with vanilla ice cream.

Kathleen Purnell
Wicomico County Unit (Salisbury)

PEPPER RELISH

2 dozen green peppers
2 dozen red peppers
2 dozen medium onions
2 cups celery, chopped

4 cups sugar
6 cups vinegar
3 tablespoons salt

Using a food grinder or processer, grind peppers and onions together. Pour into a heavy saucepan. Add boiling water to cover. Scald for five minutes. Drain and add celery, sugar, vinegar, and salt. Bring to a boil and simmer for 1/2 hour. Pour into hot sterilized jars and seal.

Rebecca Puente
Bel Air Unit (Harford)

GRANNY'S MAYONNAISE

2 eggs
2 tablespoons prepared
   mustard
1 can sweetened
   condensed Eagle Brand
   milk

Vinegar

Place all ingredients into a 1 1/2 quart bowl. Fill milk can one-half full of vinegar and one-half full of water. Stir until blended.

Carole Gregg
Garrett County Unit

International Fare

Silver Spring Acorn Dome—Marcy Shear Wolpe

This acorn dome marks the site where in 1840, Francis Blair, while horseback riding, discovered the "Silver Spring." The sun rays on the Mica particles in the spring caused Mr. Blair to name the spot and later the town "Silver Spring." The park was restored and dedicated in 1955. Drawing by Marcy Shear Wolpe, a volunteer from Montgomery County.

CHICKEN TETRAZZINI

1 (12-ounce) package thin
spaghetti, cooked tender
4 chicken bouillon cubes
3½ cups boiling water
2 (3-ounce) cans sliced
mushrooms, drained
(reserve liquid)
6 tablespoons butter or
margarine
½ teaspoon salt
¼ teaspoon pepper

⅛ teaspoon cayenne
pepper
1 cup heavy cream or
evaporated milk
4 cups chicken, cooked
and sliced
2 pimentoes, diced
¼ cup chopped parsley,
fresh or dried
3 tablespoons flour

Preheat oven to 350 degrees. Dissolve bouillon in boiling water. Add mushroom liquid. Melt butter in large saucepan, remove from heat and blend in flour, salt, pepper and cayenne. Slowly stir in bouillon mixture. Cook over low heat until sauce is thick and smooth. Remove from heat; gradually add cream. Stir 2 cups of sauce into drained spaghetti; place in a greased 3-quart casserole dish, making a wide well in the center of spaghetti for cream mixture. Stir mushrooms, chicken, pimento and parsley into remaining sauce; spoon into well in center of casserole. Sprinkle with Parmesan cheese, if desired. Bake in a moderate oven at 350 degrees for about 40 minutes or until bubbly and brown on top.

Note: 3½ cups chicken broth may be substituted for bouillon and water. Tossed green salad or Italian salad, garlic bread and dessert complete your meal! Serves 6.

Ester Lewis
Worcester County Unit (Ocean City)
Similar recipe submitted by: Harold T. Johnson
Park Heights Unit

CHICKEN CHASSEUR

1/3 cup flour
1 teaspoon salt
1/4 teaspoon oregano
1/8 teaspoon pepper
8 chicken legs
3 tablespoons margarine
2 medium tomatoes,
   peeled and diced

2/3 cup dry white wine
1 tablespoon lemon juice
1/2 cup onions, chopped
1 cup mushrooms, sliced
1 tablespoon margarine
1 teaspoon sugar
1/4 cup water

Blend together flour, salt, oregano, and pepper. Set aside 1 tablespoon of this mixture. Coat chicken in remaining flour mixture. In a heavy skillet, brown chicken in 3 tablespoons margarine. Combine wine and lemon juice; pour over chicken. Add onions; bring to a boil. Reduce heat; cover and cook over low heat for 40 to 50 minutes or until chicken is tender. In a small skillet cook mushrooms in 1 tablespoon margarine until tender. Drain. Remove cooked chicken to a platter. Keep warm. Add mushrooms, tomatoes and sugar to wine mixture in skillet. Cook until vegetables are tender (about 5 minutes). Blend together reserved 1 tablespoon flour mixture and water. Add to sauce. Cook and stir until thickened and bubbly. Pour over chicken on platter. Serves 4.

Ruth Greenfeld
Park Heights/Forest Park Unit (Baltimore)

TERIYAKI CHICKEN

1 frying chicken, cut up
1/2 cup soy sauce
1/2 cup salad oil
1/4 cup white wine

1 clove garlic, crushed
1 teaspoon ground ginger
1 tablespoon grated
   orange peel

Place chicken in a large glass bowl. Using a small bowl, mix soy sauce, oil, wine, garlic, ginger and orange peel together. Pour over chicken and place in refrigerator for 8 hours (turn once in 4 hours). Place chicken in a roasting pan and bake at 350 degrees for 1 hour, basting frequently with marinade. Serves 4.

Mrs. James Quinn
Severna Park Unit (Severna Park)

CHINESE SHRIMP IN GARLIC

Sauce:

½ cup chicken broth
2 tablespoons soy sauce
1 teaspoon salt

1 tablespoon cornstarch
2 tablespoons water

Combine broth, soy sauce, salt and cornstarch with water in a small bowl to make the sauce.

Main Dish:

2 tablespoons vegetable oil
1 small onion, chopped
1 teaspoon ginger root, grated
4 to 5 cloves garlic, sliced

5 to 6 Chinese dried black mushrooms, soak 30 minutes in warm water
1 cup peas, fresh or frozen
2 cups rice, cooked
1 pound shrimp, cooked

Heat oil in wok and stir fry onion, ginger and garlic for 1 to 2 minutes. Add mushrooms, which have been sliced, and peas; stir fry 1 to 3 minutes. Add shrimp and continue to stir fry 1 to 2 more minutes. Add sauce to wok and heat until sauce boils and has thickened. Serve immediately over hot rice. Serves 4.

Mim Kary
South County Unit (Annapolis)

TUNA CHOW MEIN

1 cup celery, chopped
¼ cup onion, chopped
2 tablespoons green
  pepper, chopped
1 tablespoon butter or
  margarine
1 (6½-ounce) can tuna,
  drained

1 (5-ounce) can chow
  mein noodles, divided
1 (10½-ounce) can
  condensed cream of
  mushroom soup
¼ cup milk
¼ cup water

In a large skillet, sauté celery, onion and green pepper in butter until onion is tender. Stir in remaining ingredients except ½ can chow mein noodles. Pour into an ungreased 1½-quart casserole. Sprinkle with reserved noodles. Bake, uncovered, at 350 degrees for 30 minutes. Serves 4.

Frances B. Garver
Montgomery County Unit (Silver Spring)

FAR EAST CHERRY AND HAM

2½ cups ham, cooked
  and cubed
2 tablespoons oil
1 (16-ounce) can chunk
  pineapple
1 (16-ounce) can light
  cherries
½ cup brown sugar
1 teaspoon prepared
  mustard

3 tablespoons vinegar
1 tablespoon soy sauce
2 tablespoons cornstarch
1 cup green and red
  peppers, cut into pieces
¾ cup onion, cut into
  chunks

Brown ham in oil. Drain pineapple and cherries, reserving liquid. Combine juices, sugar, mustard, soy sauce, vinegar, and cornstarch. Add to ham and cook until thickened. Add peppers, onion, pineapple, and cherries. Simmer for 5 to 10 minutes. Serve with rice or Chinese noodles. Serves 6 to 8.

Grace M. Snively
Washington County Unit (Hagerstown)

CHINESE EGG ROLLS

Filling:

¹/₂ pound ground pork
  or beef
¹/₂ pound bean sprouts
¹/₄ pound mushrooms,
  sliced thin
¹/₄ pound spinach,
  shredded

2 eggs, beaten
¹/₂ cup shrimp, sliced thin
3 spring onions with
  tops, sliced thin
2 tablespoons soy sauce
¹/₂ teaspoon salt or MSG
¹/₂ cup peanut oil

Using a small skillet, fry eggs as for a thin omelet. Cut into threads when done. Combine remaining filling ingredients and fry in hot peanut oil in wok for 10 minutes, stirring constantly. Combine 3 tablespoons cornstarch with 3 tablespoons water and stir paste into filling mixture. Refrigerate to use later.

Wrappers:

25 (1 box) frozen egg roll
  wrappers
1 cup peanut oil

¹/₂ cup cornstarch
¹/₂ cup water

Thaw wrappers for 1 hour; peel apart carefully to avoid splitting. Place 3 heaping tablespoons of filling into center of each roll; wrap as illustrated on egg roll box. Seal wrapper flap with a mixture of cornstarch and water. Place wrapped egg rolls into boiling peanut oil in wok; fry until golden brown. Serve hot. Makes 25.

Pao Chen Wu
Merle/Duvall Unit (Adelphi)

SLOPPY JOES

3 pounds ground beef
1 large onion, chopped
¹/₂ cup flour
1 bottle catsup (14
  ounces)

¹/₂ cup water
1 teaspoon chili powder

Cook onion and ground beef until all meat is browned. Drain. Return to pan and mix in flour. Add catsup, water, and chili powder and mix well. Bring to boil, then simmer for ¹/₂ hour or longer. Serve on hamburger rolls.

Patricia R. Amass
Carroll County Unit (Westminster)

CRAB FOO YUNG

Oil
6 eggs
3 tablespoons cornstarch
¼ pound crab meat
1 cup Hericium

caralloides,* blanched
1 stalk celery, sliced fine
1 teaspoon salt
⅛ teaspoon Accent

Beat eggs lightly with a fork. Add cornstarch and stir. Add remaining ingredients and mix well. Heat oil in a skillet to 300 degrees. Spoon a little of egg mixture into the pan to make patties 4 inches in diameter. Cook until set; turn to complete cooking. Remove from pan and drain. Repeat until all the mixture has been used. Lay the deep fried omelets in a pan; add just enough water to cover. Bring to a gentle boil. Lift the omelets out and place on a heated serving platter. Keep warm.

*Hard vegetables such as carrots

Sauce:
1 (10-ounce) can chicken
   or beef broth
2 teaspoons sugar
2 teaspoons soy sauce

Accent
1 tablespoon cornstarch
¼ cup cold water

Heat broth to boiling. Add sugar, soy sauce and Accent. Thicken with cornstarch dissolved in cold water. Pour over egg omelets and serve immediately. Serves 6.

Dr. Eugene D. Byrd, Jr.
Park Heights/Forest Park Unit (Baltimore)

NOODLE-MUSHROOM KUGEL

1 (8-ounce) package thin
noodles
3 tablespoons oil
1 1/2 cups onions, chopped
1/2 pound mushrooms,
chopped

1/2 teaspoon salt
1/8 teaspoon pepper
1/8 teaspoon garlic powder
3 eggs, beaten

Cook the noodles according to package directions. Drain well. Preheat oven to 350 degrees. Heat the oil in a 10-inch skillet and sauté the onions until they begin to brown; add mushrooms and continue to sauté for about 30 minutes. Season the onions and mushrooms with salt, pepper, and garlic powder. In a large bowl, combine the cooked noodles, the mushroom mixture, and eggs; mix well. Pour mixture into a greased 8-inch square pan and bake in a 350 degree oven for 30 minutes. Bake uncovered until crisp on top. For a softer kugel, bake covered. Serves 6 to 8.

Anita Raynes
Northwest Community Unit (Baltimore)

CHINESE BEEF WITH BROCCOLI

2 1/2 pounds flank steak,
thinly sliced
2 tablespoons cornstarch
2 tablespoons soy sauce
4 tablespoons cooking
sherry
3 tablespoons oil
1/2 cup water

2 pounds broccoli, cut
into 2 1/2 inch pieces
1 (9-ounce) can water
chestnuts, sliced
1 (9-ounce) can bamboo
shoots
2 tablespoons powdered
beef bouillon

Mix cornstarch, soy sauce, and cooking sherry in a large bowl. Add beef; stir to cover. Set aside for 1 hour. Heat oil in a skillet or wok; stir fry beef, adding 1/2 cup water while cooking. Add broccoli, water chestnuts, bamboo shoots, and beef bouillon, toss to coat vegetables and cook until broccoli has wilted but is still crisp. Serves 6 to 8.

Pat Lindsay
Frederick County Unit (Ijamsville)

PANSIT (FILIPINO DISH)

3 tablespoons oil
1 pound pork or
   chicken, cubed
1 bud garlic
1 medium onion, sliced
½ pound shrimp, cooked
1 tablespoon soy sauce
1 cube chicken bouillon
1 cup boiling water
1 (16-ounce) can French-
   cut green beans,
   drained

1 small cabbage,
   shredded
2 medium carrots,
   shredded
1 stalk celery, thinly
   sliced
Salt and Pepper

Using a large skillet or wok, sauté pork, garlic and onion until lightly browned. Stir in shrimp and soy sauce; simmer gently for 2 to 3 minutes. Dissolve bouillon in hot water and add to pan along with cabbage, carrots, and celery; cook about 5 minutes. Add beans and simmer for 5 minutes; season with salt and pepper and additional soy sauce if desired. Serve over thin spaghetti or rice. Garnish with sliced hard cooked eggs and lemon wedges. Serves 6.

Note: Once you taste this you will be doubling the recipe because the left overs taste even better! This is a good way to use leftover roasted pork or chicken.

Sue M. Eikamp
St. Mary's County Unit (Lexington Park)

Oxen in Calvert Co.

M. B. Gordon

HUNGARIAN STEW WITH NOODLES

¹/₂ cup salad oil
1 medium clove garlic
5 pounds beef stew,
cut into 1-inch cubes
4 medium onions, sliced
3 (6-ounce) cans tomato
paste
2¹/₂ cups water
1 tablespoon paprika
2 teaspoons salt

1 teaspoon pepper
1 bay leaf
2 (8-ounce) packages
bow-tie macaroni
1 tablespoon butter or
margarine
1 tablespoon minced
parsley
¹/₂ teaspoon
caraway seed

In an 8-quart Dutch oven, over medium heat, cook garlic clove in salad oil for 1 minute; discard. Add meat and onions; cook, stirring ocassionally, until meat is lightly browned. Stir in tomato paste, water, paprika, salt, pepper and bay leaf; heat to boiling. Reduce heat to low, cover; simmer 2 hours or until meat is fork-tender, stirring often. Cook macaroni according to package directions. Drain and toss gently with butter or margarine and parsley. To serve, sprinkle stew with lemon peel and caraway seed. Serve over macaroni. Serves 12.
Note: This may be frozen up to 1 month.

Mrs. Jane Driver
Howard County Unit (Mariottsville)

Woman's Club of Denton

SPINAKOPETA (SPINACH AND CHEESE PIE)

3 (8-ounce) boxes frozen
   chopped spinach,
   drained
2 tablespoons onions,
   chopped
1 pound Ricotta cheese

¹/₂ pound Feta cheese
3 eggs, slightly beaten
1 box Phyllo pastry
   dough
1 cup butter, melted

Preheat oven to 375 degrees. In a mixing bowl, combine spinach, onions, cheeses and eggs with melted butter until thoroughly blended. Set aside. Layer 10 individual sheets of phyllo, brushing each sheet with melted butter. Spread spinach mixture evenly on top. Layer 10 more buttered phyllo sheets on top. Bake for 35 to 45 minutes or until phyllo is puffed and brown. Serves 8 to 10. *Note: This dish may be prepared ahead and frozen - thaw slightly and bake.*

Mrs. Maggie Buterbaugh
Frederick County Unit (Ijamsville)

TOSTADA PIZZA

2 tablespoons corn meal
2 cups Bisquick
¹/₂ cup water
1 pound ground beef
³/₄ cup water
1 can chopped green
   chillies
1 package Taco seasoning
   mix

1 (16-ounce) can refried
   beans
1 cup Cheddar cheese,
   shredded
Lettuce, cut into bite
   sized pieces
1 onion, chopped
1 tomato, chopped
Hot sauce

Grease a pizza pan. Sprinkle the corn meal over the pan. Mix the Bisquick and ¹/₂ cup water with a fork. Roll dough on a floured surface to fit the pan. Put dough into the pizza pan; pat down and crimp the edges. Brown the meat; drain off excess fat. Add ³/₄ cup water, chillies, and Taco seasoning to meat in pan. Simmer for 15 minutes. Preheat oven to 450 degrees. Spread the refried beans over the dough; top with meat mixture. Bake for 20 minutes at 450 degrees. Top with cheese and return to oven for 3 to 4 minutes. Slice and serve with lettuce, onion, tomato and hot sauce. Serves 4 to 6.

Mary A. Shimoda
Glen Burnie Unit (Glen Burnie)

BEEF BOURGUIGNON

1/2 cup butter or margarine
2 1/2 pounds boneless beef
  chuck, cubed 1 1/2 inches
3 tablespoons brandy
1/2 pound small white
  onions, peeled
1/2 pound small fresh
  mushrooms, washed
2 1/2 tablespoons potato
  flour
2 to 2 1/2 teaspoons
  meat-extract paste*

2 tablespoons tomato
  paste
1 1/2 cups Burgundy wine
3/4 cup sherry
3/4 cup ruby port
1 (10 1/2-ounce) can
  condensed beef broth,
  undiluted
1/8 teaspoon pepper
1 bay leaf

Slowly heat a 4-quart Dutch oven with a tight-fitting lid. Add 2 tablespoons butter; heat, being careful not to burn over high heat, brown beef cubes well all over, about 1/4 at a time. Lift out beef as it browns. Continue until all beef is browned, adding more butter as needed. Return all beef to Dutch oven. In a small saucepan, heat 2 tablespoons brandy just until vapor rises, ignite; pour over beef. As flame dies, remove beef cubes and set aside. Melt 2 tablespoons butter in Dutch oven over low heat. Add onions and cook, covered, until onions brown lightly. Add mushrooms and cook, stirring, for 3 minutes. Remove from heat. Stir in flour, meat-extract paste, and tomato paste until well-blended. Stir in Burgundy, sherry, port, and beef broth. Pre-heat oven to 350 degrees. Bring wine mixture to a boil; stir; remove from heat. Add beef, pepper, and bay leaf. Mix well. Bake, covered for 1 1/2 hours or until beef is tender, stirring as necessary. Gradually add remaining brandy. Serves 6 to 8.

*Note: *Do not use liquid meat extract. This dish is better if made the day before and refrigerated overnight. Reheat gently before serving. If necessary, add a little wine to thin the sauce.*

Mrs. W.N. Valk (Fayann)
Towson Unit (Baltimore)

FISH DISH ITALIAN

1 large onion, chopped	2 bay leaves, crumbled
1 clove garlic, minced	1/4 teaspoon cinnamon
3 tablespoons olive oil	1/4 teaspoon oregano
1 (6-ounce) can tomato paste	1 cup red wine
	Salt and pepper to taste
1 (8-ounce) can tomato sauce	2 pounds fish fillets, fresh or frozen

Sauté onions and garlic in oil until tender. Add remaining ingredients, except fish. Simmer sauce for 15 minutes until thick and smooth. Preheat oven to 350 degrees. Place fish fillets in a 12-x-8-x-2 inch glass baking dish. Pour sauce over fish. Bake at 350 for 30 minutes or until fish flakes easily with a fork. Garnish with ripe olives. Serves 6.

Liz Barclay
Annapolis Unit (Annapolis)

CITY DOCK, ANNAPOLIS
DAVID MOREHEAD

SHRIMP ROMA

1 clove garlic
1 medium onion, sliced
3 tablespoons olive oil
1 tablespoon butter
1 pound shrimp, peeled
and deveined
3 (8-ounce) cans tomato
sauce

^{1}/$_2$ teaspoon salt
1 teaspoon dried oregano
1 teaspoon parsley
1 box shell noodles,
prepared according to
directions

Sauté garlic and onion in olive oil and butter until tender. Add shrimp and cook for 2 minutes. Add tomato sauce, salt, oregano and parsley. Simmer for 5 minutes and serve over hot noodles. Serves 6.

Jan O'Malley
Oxon Hill/Clinton Unit (Clinton)

Main Dishes

Montpelier Mansion

Montpelier Mansion

This 18th century home of the Thomas Snowden family, has been pointed to as one of the most beautiful Georgian houses in America. The Snowdens were once extensive land holders—at one time owning 20,000 acres, near the head of the South River (Rts. 301 and 50). The house and grounds have now been presented to the Maryland-National Capital Park and Planning Commission, in order to preserve the historic significance of the property. "Friends of Montpelier" are currently striving to help furnish the mansion. Plans are now underway to restore the beautiful boxwood garden.

CHIPPED BEEF CREOLE

1 large can evaporated
milk
1 tablespoon flour
¼ pound air-dried beef,
chopped or shredded
1 tablespoon
Worcestershire sauce
1 tablespoon cooking
sherry
¼ cup butter
½ cup chopped celery

½ cup chopped onions
1 medium green pepper,
chopped
¼ pound fresh
mushrooms, sliced
1 (8-ounce) can tomato
sauce
½ cup cold water
¼ teaspoon cream of
tartar

Scald milk in medium-sized double boiler, thicken with flour mixed with 2 tablespoons water, stir until thickened. Add dried beef, Worcestershire sauce and sherry. Turn off heat under double-boiler and let stand. In medium-sized skillet, melt butter and sauté celery, onions, green pepper, and mushrooms until tender. Add to double boiler. In same skillet, heat tomato sauce mixed with water and cream of tartar. Allow to cool to approximate temperature of contents of double boiler. Slowly combine the two mixtures, stirring constantly and mixing well. Serve over hot, fluffy rice. Yield: 4 to 6 servings.

Louise B. Compton
Merle Duvall Unit (Hyattsville)

EASY COMPANY STEW

3 pounds stewing beef
1 can cream of mushroom
soup
1 can cream of chicken
soup
1 can cream of celery
soup

1 soup can dry red wine
½ package instant onion
soup mix
½ pound fresh mushrooms
Rice or noodles

Combine first 6 ingredients. Bake 5 hours at 300 degrees or 8 hours in a crock pot on low. During last ½ hour, add fresh mushrooms. Serve stew over cooked rice or noodles. Wonderful flavor!

Pat Behenna
Laurel/Beltsville Unit (Laurel)

REUBEN BAKE

1 (8-ounce) package
noodles
2 tablespoons margarine
1 (1-pound) can
sauerkraut
1 (12-ounce) can corned
beef
1/2 cup Thousand Island
dressing

2 tomatoes, sliced
2 cups shredded Swiss
cheese
1/2 cup crushed rye
crackers
1/4 teaspoon caraway seeds
2 tablespoons melted
butter

Preheat oven to 350 degrees. Cook noodles, drain and toss with 2 tablespoons margarine. Place noodles in bottom of greased baking dish (12-x-8-x-2), top with sauerkraut and shredded corned beef. Spread dressing over corned beef and top with tomato slices. Sprinkle with the Swiss cheese. Crush rye crackers and toss with 2 tablespoons melted butter and caraway seeds and sprinkle over top. Bake for 35 minutes at 350 degrees. Yield: 6 to 8 servings.

Ruth M. Durst
Garrett County Unit (Oakland)

SWEET AND SOUR TONGUE

3 to 4 pound fresh beef
tongue
4 medium onions, sliced
2 tablespoons butter or
margarine
2 heaping tablespoons
flour

Beef stock from tongue
10 gingersnaps
2 thinly sliced lemons
3/4 cup raisins
3/4 to 1 pound dark
brown sugar

Place tongue in large pot. Add sliced onions and cover with water. Bring to boil, cover and simmer for 2 1/2 to 3 hours until tender. Remove skin while hot. Brown flour in butter. Place gingershaps in a bowl and add enough stock to dissolve snaps. Combine with flour and butter and add more stock for gravy consistency. Add lemons, raisins, brown sugar. Slice tongue and heat in sauce. Yield: 6 to 8 servings.

Nancy F. Gideon
Annapolis Unit (Annapolis)

SWEET AND SOUR STEW

2 medium-sized packages
of stew meat, cubed
Cooking oil
2 1/2 quarts water
3 large diced potatoes
3 large diced carrots
2 stalks celery

1 medium onion, diced
1/2 cup white vinegar
1 cup catsup
1 tablespoon
Worcestershire sauce
1 cup brown sugar

Put small amount of cooking oil in skillet and brown meat; drain off excess fat. Put meat and 2 1/2 quarts of water in large pot and add diced vegetables. Simmer until almost tender, about 20 minutes. Add remaining ingredients and continue to simmer for 1 hour. Serves 4.

Mrs. Judith Ann Bittinger
Garrett County Unit (Oakland)

BEEF WITH SOUR CREAM

1 pound lean beef round
steak
1/4 cup flour seasoned with
salt, pepper, and
garlic powder
2 tablespoons vegetable
oil
3/4 cup chopped onions
1 cup beef broth

1/2 teaspoon thyme
1 (4-ounce) can sliced
mushrooms and liquid
1 (10-ounce) package
frozen green peas
1/2 cup sour cream
3 to 4 cups hot cooked
rice or noodles

Remove bone and fat from steak. Cut meat into thin, narrow strips. Dredge in flour. Using a large skillet (electric skillet works best), quickly brown meat on all sides in hot oil. Add onions, broth, thyme, and liquid from mushrooms. Cover and simmer broth about 45 minutes or until meat is tender. Add mushrooms and peas. Cover and cook 5 to 7 minutes. Stir in sour cream. Heat but DO NOT boil. Serve over hot rice or noodles. Yield: 6 servings.
Note: Cook peas before adding to the meat, then you will be sure they are completely cooked.

Mrs. Sharon L. Martin
Carroll County Unit (Hampstead)

BEEF STEW

2 tablespoons olive oil
2 slices bacon, chopped
1/2 cup chopped onion
1/2 cup sliced celery
1 clove garlic, minced
1 1/2 pounds lean stew beef, cut into 1-inch cubes
2 tablespoons chopped parsley
1 (16-ounce) can peeled tomatoes, broken up
1 cup water
1 teaspoon beef broth granules
1/2 teaspoon dried sweet basil, crumbled
Salt and pepper
1/2 teaspoon sugar
3 medium carrots, peeled and sliced
3 medium potatoes, peeled and diced
1 1/2 cups peas (frozen or canned)

Heat the oil in an electric skillet. Add the bacon and sauté until crisp. Remove the bacon from the pan with a slotted spoon and reserve. Add the onion, celery, and garlic and sauté for 5 minutes. Remove with a slotted spoon and reserve. Add the beef and cook over moderate heat until well browned on all sides, turning often. Add all the reserved ingredients, parsley, tomatoes, water, beef broth granules and seasonings and cook, covered, over low heat for 1 hour. Add the carrots and potatoes and stir well. Cover and cook for 45 minutes. Add peas and stir well. Cook another 15 minutes or until vegetables are tender. (Thicken with flour and cold water if desired.)

Brenda Earley
South County Unit (Shady Side)

MABLE'S MEATLOAF

2 pounds ground beef
1/2 cup bread crumbs
2 eggs
1/2 teaspoon salt
1/3 teaspoon pepper
1/2 cup Italian sauce or catsup
1 envelope Lipton's Onion Soup mix
1 tablespoon soy sauce

Preheat oven to 400 degrees. Combine all ingredients; mix well. Shape into a loaf and cook in a greased 9-x-5-x-3-inch loaf pan. Bake for 30 to 45 minutes. Serves 4 to 6.

Drs. Adams and Ashford
Rosemont/Edmondson Unit (Baltimore)

SPAGHETTI WITH MEAT BALLS

1 package spaghetti
1/2 green pepper, chopped
1 onion, chopped
1/2 teaspoon salt

1/2 teaspoon pepper
1/2 teaspoon season-all
2 pounds ground beef
1 jar spaghetti sauce

Cook spaghetti until tender. Mix green pepper, onion, salt and pepper and seaon-all together in skillet and brown with ground beef. Add jar of sauce and simmer for 20 minutes. Mix with drained, cooked spaghetti.

Mrs. Marguerite Anderson
Park Heights/Forest Park Unit (Baltimore)

Variation: Cheese sauce: 1/2 cup butter, 1/3 cup flour, 1 1/2 teaspoons salt, 1 cup water, 2 cups *undiluted* evaporated milk, 2 cups shredded American cheese, and 1/3 cup grated Parmesan cheese. Melt butter, add flour and 1 1/2 teaspoons salt. Add the 1 cup water and evaporated milk slowly; cook over medium heat until thickened. Add cheeses. Layer spaghetti, spaghetti sauce, and cheese sauce alternately in two 13-x-9-x-2-inch casserole dishes. Bake at 350 degrees for 15 to 25 minutes.

Mrs. Ann Roberts
Southern Charles County Unit (LaPlata)

Variation: To make your own spaghetti sauce and meatballs: 3 tablespoons cooking oil, 2 cloves garlic, 1 medium chopped onion, 1 medium chopped green pepper, 1/2 teaspoon marjoram, 1/2 teaspoon thyme, 1/2 teaspoon parsley flakes, 1 teaspoon celery flakes, 1 teapoon oregano, 2 (6-ounce) cans tomato paste, 2 (32-ounce) jars Ragu Spaghetti Sauce with Mushrooms. Brown garlic in oil in large heavy saucepan; remove from pan, then sauté onion and green pepper in same pan. Add spices and stir to combine. Add tomato paste and simmer 5 minutes, stirring often. Add Ragu sauce and stir in paste and sauce cans of water. Simmer slowly 3 to 4 hours. Add water to sauce as needed when it becomes too thick. Meatballs: Combine the following ingredients in a large bowl-3 pounds ground beef, 1 medium finely chopped onion, 1 medium finely chopped green pepper, 1/2 teaspoon jarjoram, 1/2 teaspoon thyme, 1/2 teaspoon parsley flakes, 1 teaspoon oregano, 1/4 teaspoon minced garlic, 4 eggs, 1/2 cold water, 1 1/2 cups bread crumbs, 1/4 cup Parmesan cheese, 1/4 teaspoon salt, and 1/4 teaspoon pepper. Form into small balls and brown in a little oil. Drop into spaghetti sauce and simmer about 1¹/₂ hours. Serve over cooked spaghetti, rigatoni, or any pasta you prefer. *Note: Sprinkle Parmesan cheese to taste on pasta before putting on sauce.*

Mrs. Linda Palmer
Worcester County Unit (Berlin)

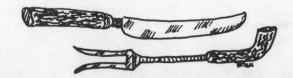

HAMBURGER AND MACARONI CASSEROLE

¹/₂ **pound fresh mushrooms**	1 **teaspoon salt**
1 **onion, chopped**	¹/₂ **teaspoon oregano**
¹/₂ **green pepper, chopped**	¹/₄ **teaspoon pepper**
2 **tablespoons salad oil**	1 **cup uncooked macaroni**
1¹/₂ **pounds ground beef**	1 **small can tomatoes**

Sauté mushrooms, onion and green pepper in oil. Add ground beef and cook until browned. Add remaining ingredients. Put in baking dish and bake at 350 degrees for 45 minutes.

Sylvia M. Gorban
Montgomery County (Silver Spring)

Variations: Add 1 (1 pound, 1-ounce) can cream-style corn, 1 envelope onion soup mix or ¹/₂ cup shredded Cheddar cheese.

Elois B. Reynolds
Somerset County (Princess Anne)
Ann Harrison Ryder
Howard County (Ellicott City)

For Hamburger Heaven: Brown ground beef in skillet and stir in 1 (15-ounce) can tomato sauce. Mix 1 (8-ounce) cream cheese, 1 cup sour cream, and 1 medium chopped onion together. Cook 1 (8-ounce) package spinach noodles or egg noodles; drain. Layer noodles, cheese-onion mixture and beef until used up. Top with 1 cup shredded mozzarella cheese and bake as above.

Nancy Dick
Kent County Unit (Chestertown)

GIGI'S SPECIAL

3 pounds ground beef
5 onions, chopped
1 whole garlic, chopped
1 tablespoon salt, divided
1 tablespoon pepper, divided
1/4 cup oil
1 tablespoon garlic salt, divided

1 can tomatoes
18 ounces tomato sauce
6 ounces tomato paste
1 (16-ounce) package macaroni
16 ounces American cheese

Place ground beef, onions and garlic in oil in a large skillet. Sprinkle with 1 teaspoon salt, pepper, and garlic salt and brown. Drain off excess fat. Mash tomatoes. Add tomatoes, tomato sauce and tomato paste to ground beef mixture in a 4 quart saucepan. Add 2 teaspoons salt and pepper and 1 1/4 teaspoons garlic salt. Simmer for 1 1/2 hours. Cook macaroni as directed on package. Drain. Place a layer of macaroni in loaf pan, cover with sauce, then place a layer of cheese. Repeat layers. Bake for 35 minutes at 350 degrees.

Note: This dish can be prepared ahead of time and frozen. When ready to use, let thaw and then bake as directed.

Sandra Ann Roberts
Southern Charles County Unit (La Plata)

QUICHE LORRAINE

1 (9-inch) pie shell, unbaked
12 slices bacon, fried crisp and crumbled
1 cup shredded Swiss cheese

1/3 cup minced onion
4 eggs
2 cups half and half
3/4 teaspoon salt
1/4 teaspoon sugar

Preheat oven to 400 degrees. Sprinkle bacon, cheese and onion in bottom of pie shell. Beat eggs with rotary beater along with half and half, salt, sugar. Pour over bacon and cheese. Bake at 400 degrees for 10 minutes, reduce heat to 350 degrees for 40 minutes. Insert knife in center-knife should come out clean. Let stand for 10 minutes before cutting.

Mary Lou Clem
Northern Charles County Unit (Oxon Hill)

POOR MAN'S OMELET

6 eggs	1 teaspoon salt
1 teaspoon Angostura aromatic bitters	¼ teaspoon pepper
	¼ cup butter or margarine
3 slices stale bread	Parsley Sauce
½ cup milk	

Separate eggs. Beat egg yolks until thick; beat in bitters. In a small bowl, crumble bread and pour in milk. Let stand until milk is absorbed. Fold bread, salt and pepper into egg yolks. Beat egg whites until stiff and fold into egg yolk mixture. Heat butter until bubbly brown in a 10-inch skillet. Pour in egg mixture when butter sizzles. Cook without stirring until bottom of omelet is golden brown. Place skillet under broiler and broil for a few minutes until top is slightly browned. Fold omelet in half. Place on a platter. Spoon Parsley Sauce over. Yield: 4 servings.

Parsley Sauce:

¼ cup butter or margarine	⅓ cup finely chopped parsley
¼ cup flour	
2 cups milk	1 tablespoon lemon juice
1 teaspoon Angostura aromatic bitters	Salt and pepper to taste

Melt butter. Stir in flour. Gradually stir in milk and bitters. Stir over low heat until sauce bubbles and thickens. Stir in parsley, lemon juice, salt and pepper. Simmer for another 2 minutes. Spoon over omelet. Makes 2 cups.

Agnes Beck
Oxon Hill/Clinton Unit (Oxon Hill)

QUICHE A LA SUISSE

1 large onion, sliced thin
3/4 stick of butter
6 slices bacon, cubed and
fried crisp
6 eggs
1 1/2 cups light cream
1/2 pound shredded
Gruyere cheese
1 teaspoon salt

2 green onions, chopped,
including stems
1 teaspoon marjoram
1 teaspoon chopped
parsley
1 teaspoon chopped
chives
1 (10-inch) pie shell,
unbaked

Sauté onion until golden brown in butter. Beat eggs with cream. Add cheese, salt, green onions, marjoram, parsley, and chives. Add sautéed onion and drained bacon. Pour into pie shell. Bake in moderately hot oven (375 to 400 degrees) for 30 to 45 minutes or until silver knife inserted into center comes out clean.

Dr. Gloria L. Hastings
Bel Air Unit (Bel Air)

VEGETABLE QUICHE

2 tablespoons oil
1 onion, sliced
1 clove garlic, crushed
1 green pepper, chopped
4 cups broccoli and
cauliflower pieces
4 to 6 eggs, beaten
2 cups sharp Cheddar
cheese, shredded

1/2 teaspoon sea salt
1/2 teaspoon cumin
1/2 teaspoon basil or
marjoram
Optional: Sprinkle of
curry powder

Preheat oven to 325 degrees. Heat a skillet on medium heat. Add oil and vegetables; sauté lightly. Cover and steam vegetables in their own juices for 2 minutes. Fold in eggs, cheese, salt and herbs. Pour into an oiled 1 1/2-or 2-quart baking dish. Bake for 30 to 40 minutes or until set. Serves 6.

Grace O'Brien
St. Mary's County Unit (California)

GAYMER'S OLDE ENGLISH RESOLUTION ROAST

1 ounce drippings
1/2 pound small onions, peeled
2 pounds potatoes, peeled and halved
1 pound carrots, peeled and sliced
1 tablespoon plain flour
1/2 teaspoon dried rosemary

Salt and pepper to taste
4 pound shoulder of lamb
1 green pepper, cut in thin strips
1/4 pound button mushrooms
3/4 pint Gaymer's Old English Cyder

Melt drippings in roasting pan. Add onions, potatoes, and carrots and fry gently for 2 to 3 minutes. Season flour and rub into skin on shoulder to crispen it. Add strips of green pepper and mushrooms to other vegetables in pan and arrange around meat. Rub rosemary on the meat then pour cider over the vegetables. Cover with foil and roast at 400 degrees for 30 minutes; then reduce heat to 375 degrees for 1 hour and 35 minutes.

Patricia Ryan
Havre de Grace/Aberdeen Unit

"BLACK SUPREME" HOG MAWS AND CHITTERLINGS

10 pounds chitterlings
5 pounds hog maws
1/2 cup vinegar
Salt to taste
Pinch of baking soda (for tenderness)
2 large Spanish onions
3 tablespoons seafood seasoning
1 bay leaf

Dash of crushed red pepper
Dash of sage
1 tablespoon poultry seasoning
1 bunch scallions, chopped
1 large white potato (to curtail cooking odor)

Clean the chitterlings and maws. Pull out all fat. Cook slowly for 4 hours in vinegar, salt and baking soda. Skim all fat after this process. Add remaining ingredients and continue to cook slowly 1 1/2 hours longer. Serve with potato salad, rice, or green vegetables such as collard greens or fresh string beans.

Marjorie F. Ferguson
Park Heights/Forest Park Unit (Baltimore)

SAUERKRAUT-SAUSAGE STUFFED PEPPERS

6 medium green peppers
1 (1-pound) can
  sauerkraut
1/2 cup minced green
  pepper
2 tablespoons brown
  sugar
1/4 cup catsup or
  barbecue sauce
1 tart medium apple,
  peeled and cubed

1 chicken bouillon cube
1 1/2 cups water
Salt and pepper to taste
1 pound pork sausage meat
Seasoned fine dry
  bread crumbs
Grated Parmesan or
  Swiss cheese
Paprika

Cut off tops of peppers. Remove seeds. Wash and parboil peppers in boiling water for 4 minutes. Drain. Drain sauerkraut and put in cold water for 15 minutes. Squeeze dry between hands. Put in saucepan with minced pepper, brown sugar, catsup, apple, bouillon cube, water and salt and pepper. Simmer, covered, for 30 minutes. Cook sausage. Drain off fat and mince sausage with a fork to separate. Combine with sauerkraut mixture. Spoon into pepper shells. Sprinkle with bread crumbs, grated cheese and paprika. Arrange in baking dish. Pour in 1/2 cup water. Bake in preheated 350 degree oven for about 30 minutes. Yield: 6 servings.

Barbara Benussi
Dorchester County Unit (Woolford)

PORK CHOP CASSEROLE

6 pork chops
3 tablespoons oil
3 large potatoes, sliced
1 (10 1/2-ounce) can cream
  of chicken soup

2 large carrots, sliced
1 large onion, sliced
1 (16-ounce) can peas
  (optional)
1 soup can water

Brown pork chops in electric skillet in oil. Place potatoes, onion and carrots in layers over pork chops. Pour soup and water over all. Cover and simmer about 1 hour. Peas may be added for a complete dinner in a skillet. Serves 4 to 6.

Daisy Doughney
Dundalk/Patapsco Unit (Baltimore)

MOTHER DYSON'S ST. MARY'S COUNTY STUFFED HAM

12 pounds country cured
  ham
6 pounds cabbage
3 pounds onions
1 pound kale

2 tablespoons celery seed
Salt and black pepper
  to taste
Red pepper to taste

Blanche kale, chop together with cabbage and onions (food processor or blender would be helpful for this). Mix together and add seasonings. Cut deep slits in ham, opposite from the way it is usually sliced. (Ham could also be boned). Pack as much of the vegetables as possible into the slits. Put extra on top of ham. Wrap in clean cheesecloth (or pillow case) and tie securely. Cook in a large pot at least 4 hours-start timing when water begins to simmer. Use rack in bottom of pot to prevent ham from sticking. Cool before unwrapping and slicing. Juice from pot is excellent for seasoning vegetables.

Marie Dyson
St. Marys County Unit (Great Mills)

Variation: May add watercress and spring onions to other greens. 2 tablespoons celery seed and 3 tablespoons sage may be added to seasonings.
Note: The mixture should be highly seasoned, you may want to add more red pepper, salt, or sage, as the seasoning will soak into the ham.

Ann Roberts
Southern Charles County Unit (LaPlata)

ORANGE AND HAM ROLL-UPS

Rolls:

1 large can mandarin
  oranges, drained
1 1/2 cups cooked rice
1/3 cup mayonnaise or
  salad dressing
2 tablespoons chopped
  pecans

2 tablespoons parsley,
  chopped
1 tablespoon green onion,
  minced
8 slices baked ham

Chop half can of mandarin oranges. Add to rice, mayonnaise, pecans, parsley and onions. Mix well. Divide mixture into 8 portions and spoon each on a slice of ham. Roll ham and place seam side down in a greased 12-x-8-x-2-inch pan.

Sauce:

1/4 cup orange marmalade
1 teaspoon lemon juice
1/4 teaspoon ground ginger

Remainder of mandarin
oranges, left whole

Mix all ingredients and drizzle over ham rolls. Bake uncovered at 350 degrees for 25 to 30 minutes. Yield: 4 to 6 servings.
Note: This is a delicious brunch dish but is good as main dish for any meal.

Mrs. Dorothy R. Kraybill
Montgomery County Unit (Rockville)

SAUSAGE CASSEROLE

2 pounds pork sausage,
  hot or mild
1/2 teaspoon sage
2 (16-ounce) cans
  applesauce

3/4 teaspoon cinnamon
1 teaspoon nutmeg

In a large bowl, blend sausage and sage thoroughly. Form into balls. Brown balls lightly in skillet, place in medium-sized casserole dish. Blend applesauce with cinnamon and nutmeg. Pour mixture over sausage balls and bake in a 350-degree oven for 45 minutes. Yield: 6 to 8 servings.

Mrs. Millicent Long
Communities United Unit

APPLE GLAZE SPARERIBS

1 (15-ounce) jar
   unsweetened
   applesauce
¼ cup dark corn syrup
¼ cup cider vinegar
½ teaspoon powdered
   ginger

½ teaspoon powdered
   mustard
4 pounds spareribs, cut in
   serving pieces

Mix applesauce, corn syrup, vinegar, ginger and mustard. Marinate ribs in mixture for 3 hours. Remove ribs; place on foil-lined cookie sheet. Bake at 350 degrees for 1½ hours, turning occasionally and basting with marinade sauce. Serve with tossed salad and your favorite hot bread. Yield: 4 servings.

Margaret Quillen
Worcester County (Berlin)

Variation: Sweet and Sour Ribs: Pour ¼ cup vinegar and ½ cup water over the meat and let simmer 15 minutes. Mix 2 tablespoons sugar and ¼ cup soy sauce together and pour over meat. Continue cooking 15 to 20 minutes longer. Just before serving, add chunks of pineapple, onion, green pepper, and celery. Mix 2 tablespoons cornstarch with water to make a thin paste and pour over meat and vegetables, stirring constantly. Let simmer 5 minutes to thicken. Serve with rice.

Mary A. Shimoda
Glen Burnie Unit (Glen Burnie)

PORK CHOP-APPLE CASSEROLE

6 pork loin or rib chops,
cut ¾ to 1 inch thick
2 tablespoons salad oil
1¼ teaspoons salt, divided
⅛ teapoon pepper
2 cups soft breadcrumbs
½ cup firmly packed
brown sugar

½ cup sugar
3 tablespoons all-purpose
flour
½ teaspoon ground
cinnamon
6 cups sliced apples

Brown pork chops in oil. Pour off drippings, and reserve ¼ cup. Season chops with 1 teaspoon salt and pepper. Combine breadcrumbs, ¼ cup drippings, and ¼ teaspon salt. Combine sugars, flour and cinnamon; add to apples, mixing well. Place half of breadcrumbs in a 2-quart casserole or baking dish. Spoon half of apples over crumbs, and arrange pork chops on apples. Place remaining apples on chops. Cover tightly and bake for 40 minutes at 350 degree. Remove cover and top with remaining bread crumbs. Bake 10 minutes longer. Yield: 6 servings.

Mrs. Mary P. Owens
Howard County Unit (Ellicott City)

LEA'S CORDON BLEU

3 large chicken breasts,
boned and halved
lengthwise
6 thin slices boiled ham
6 ounces Swiss cheese
¼ cup flour
2 tablespoons margarine
1 cup water, divided

1 tablespoon chicken
flavored gravy
1 (3-ounce) jar sliced
mushrooms, drained
⅓ cup Sauterne
2 tablespoons all-purpose
flour
Toasted sliced almonds

Place chicken pieces on board and pound into cutlets; salt. Place ham and cheese slices on each cutlet. Roll and tie at bottom and top to keep closed. Coat with flour; brown in margarine. Place in a 13-x-9-x-2-inch baking pan. In a skillet, combine ½ cup water, gravy, and mushrooms. Pour over chicken. Cover and bake at 350 degrees for 1 to 1¼ hours. Blend 2 tablespoons flour with ½ cup cold water and Sauterne and add to gravy in baking pan. Garnish with almonds. Yield: 6 servings.

Lea LaParle
Allegany County Unit (Cumberland)

WANDA'S HAM AND CHICKEN JAMBALAYA

1 broiler-fryer (about 2½ pounds)	1 tablespoon salt
2 cups water	¼ teaspoon pepper
	1 bay leaf

Place chicken in a large kettle or Dutch oven; add water, salt, pepper and bay leaf; bring to boiling; reduce heat and cover. Simmer 45 minutes, or until chicken is tender; remove chicken from broth; reserve broth.

2 large onions, chopped (about 2 cups)	½ teaspoon leaf thyme, crumbled
¼ cup margarine	¼ teaspoon cayenne pepper
1 pound cooked ham, cubed	1 cup uncooked regular rice (may substitute 1 cup of minute rice)
1 (1 pound 12-ounce) can tomatoes, crushed	
1 large green pepper, halved, seeded, and chopped	

Sauté onions and garlic in margarine until soft in large kettle or Dutch oven; add ham, tomatoes, green pepper, thyme, cayenne and reserved chicken and broth. Heat to boiling; stir in rice; reduce heat; cover. Simmer, following rice label directions for cooking. Serve in large bowls. Serve with crusty French bread, if you wish. Yield: 8 servings.

Mrs. Wanda Creighton
Dorchester County Unit (Cambridge)

FRUIT AND NUT CHICKEN

1 Perdue chicken, cut in
  serving pieces
2 tablespoons oil
1 1/2 cups orange juice

1 teaspoon salt
1/4 teaspoon cinnamon
1/2 cup golden raisins
1/2 cup slivered almonds

Brown chicken in oil in frying pan at medium heat approximately 15 minutes each side. Pour orange juice over chicken. Sprinkle salt, cinnamon, raisins and almonds on chicken. Cover and simmer for approximately 30 minutes or until done. Yield: 4 servings.

Betty Jane Dashiell
Wicomico County Unit (Salisbury)

CHICKEN FONTINA

1/2 cup butter or margarine
6 chicken breasts or 1
  cut up chicken
1/2 teaspoon salt
1/4 teaspoon pepper
1/2 teaspoon paprika

1 lemon
1 tablespoon dehydrated
  onion
1 cup shredded Cheddar
  or Fontina cheese

Melt butter in 12-x-8-x-2-inch glass baking dish. Roll chicken pieces in butter as you place them in the dish. Sprinkle with salt, pepper, and paprika. Bake for 30 minutes at 400 degrees. Remove from oven and squeeze juice of lemon over each piece along with dehydrated onion. Cover with aluminum foil. Bake 30 minutes more then sprinkle with cheese; cover again; let cheese melt and serve.

Sis LeGates
Talbot County Unit (Easton)

Variation: Chicken Monte Carlo: Steam chicken breasts and slice thin. Place chicken in casserole along with 2 packages of frozen cooked broccoli. Make sauce using 1/3 cup butter, 1/2 cup flour, and 2-3/4 cups chicken stock (add coffee cream if necessary); cook until thickened and pour over chicken and broccoli. Add 1/2 pound sliced, sautéed mushrooms and sprinkle heavily with Parmesan cheese. Bake at 350 degrees until bubbly, about 30 minutes.

Mrs. Ethel Barr
Queen Anne County Unit (Stevensville)

COMPANY CHICKEN

1 package sliced ham
1 package sliced cheese
6 chicken breasts, boned
1 can cream of chicken
  soup

Paprika
Dash of salt and pepper

Place a slice of ham and a slice of cheese on each chicken breast and roll up. Place chicken rolls in a greased casserole dish. Pour chicken soup over chicken rolls. Sprinkle with paprika. Bake in a 325-degree oven for one hour. Serves 6.

Leola M. Dorsey
Howard County (Jessup)

Variation: Company Chicken Casserole: Use 1 can cream of mushroom soup, 1 can cream of chicken soup, 1 can cream of celery soup plus 1 soup can of water and 1 cup regular rice. Mix and pour into a large baking dish; place chicken breasts on top. Combine 1/4 cup melted butter, 1 teaspoon lemon juice and 2 teaspoons sugar and dribble over chicken. Cover and bake 1 1/2 hours at 350 degrees.
Note: May need to add a little water or chicken broth if rice gets too dry.

Daphne B. Walston
Howard County Unit (Columbia)

GLAZED CHICKEN

1 envelope Lipton onion
  soup mix
1 bottle Wishbone
  Russian dressing
1 (8-ounce) jar apricot
  preserves

Salt and pepper
2 1/2 to 3 pounds cut-up
  chicken

Mix together onion soup, dressing and preserves in a bowl. Dip chicken that has been salted and peppered into mix, covering generously. Place on a baking sheet that has been lined with foil and bake in a 350-degree oven for 1 hour.

Emma Scarborough
Worcester County Unit (Girdletree)

MARYLAND OVEN BARBECUED CHICKEN

2 frying chickens, cut
  into serving portions
1 tablespoon salt
6 tablespoons sugar
1 (6-ounce) can tomato
  paste
6 tablespoons
  Worcestershire sauce

1 large onion, diced
1 tablespoon mustard
1/2 teaspoon Tabasco sauce
1/2 cup vinegar
1/2 cup bell pepper, diced
1 (20-ounce) can
  tomatoes
1 cup water

Arrange chicken in baking pan. Mix remaining ingredients in a sauce pan and bring to a boil. Pour over chicken. Marinate for 3 hours. Bake at 350 degrees for 1 1/2 hours. Yield: 8 generous servings.
Note: For a dinner party, this recipe can be made ahead of time and frozen.

Mrs. Ruth White
North Central Unit (Baltimore)

SAVORY CRESCENT CHICKEN SQUARES

1 (3-ounce) package
  cream cheese, softened
3 tablespoons margarine,
  melted
2 cups cooked, cubed
  chicken meat
1/4 teaspoon salt
1/8 teaspoon pepper
2 tablespoons milk

1 tablespoon chopped
  chives or onion
1 tablespoon chopped
  pimiento
1 (8-ounce) can crescent
  rolls, Italian or rye
3/4 cup crushed seasoned
  croutons

Preheat oven to 350 degrees. Blend softened cream cheese and 2 tablespoons margarine until smooth. Add chicken, salt, pepper, milk, chives or onion and pimiento. Mix well. Separate rolls into 4 rectangles; seal perforations. Spoon 1/2 cup chicken mixture onto center of reach rectangle. Pull 4 corners of dough to center of mixture; seal. Brush tops with 1 tablespoon margarine. Dip in 3/4 cup crushed croutons. Bake on ungreased cookie sheet for 20 to 25 minutes until golden brown. Yield: 4 servings.

Linda Blachly
Merle Duvall Unit (Hyattsville)

CHICKEN DIVAN

2 (10-ounce) packages
frozen broccoli
(may use fresh)
3 to 4 large chicken
breasts, cooked and
boned
2 cans cream of chicken
soup

$\frac{1}{2}$ cup mayonnaise
1 tablespoon lemon juice
$\frac{1}{2}$ teaspoon curry powder
$\frac{1}{2}$ cup sharp cheese,
shredded
$\frac{1}{2}$ cup bread crumbs
1 tablespoon melted
margarine

Cook broccoli in boiling salted water until tender. Drain. Arrange in greased 12-x-8-x-2-inch glass baking dish. Arrange chicken on top. Combine soup, mayonnaise, lemon juice and curry powder; pour over chicken. Sprinkle combined bread crumbs and melted margarine over all. Bake at 350 degrees for 25 to 30 minutes or until thoroughly heated. This may be frozen, if desired, and baked later.

Kathy Eiswert
Garrett County Unit (Oakland)

CHICKEN SURPRISE

1 whole chicken
1 (10-$\frac{3}{4}$-ounce) can cream
of mushroom soup
1 soup can milk
$\frac{1}{2}$ teaspoon salt
$\frac{1}{2}$ teaspoon pepper

1 (10 to 16-ounce) can
peas
1 cup mushrooms
(fresh preferred)
1 large bag potato chips

Boil and bone the chicken. In blender, mix mushroom soup and 1 can of milk. Stir in the salt and pepper. Drain peas, then add peas and mushrooms to the sauce. Layer a 12-x-8-x-2-inch baking dish with the chicken, then the potato chips, then continue to alternate layers until the pan is full. Pour the mushroom sauce over the layers. Bake at 350 degrees for 30 minutes. A delicious surprise!

JoAnne Zwick
Southern Charles County Unit (Waldorf)

TROPICAL CHICKEN-HAWAIIAN STYLE

2 fryer chickens, cut into serving pieces
1 1/2 teaspoons salt
1 egg, slightly beaten
1 (6-ounce) can frozen pineapple juice concentrate, thawed and undiluted

1 1/2 cups fine dry bread crumbs
1/4 cup margarine, melted
1 1/2 cups flaked coconut

Rinse chicken pieces; pat dry with paper towel. Sprinkle salt over chicken. In pie plate combine beaten egg and pineapple concentrate. In a separate pie plate combine bread crumbs with the melted margarine; add coconut and mix well. Coat chicken pieces with the pineapple mixture then roll in the coconut bread crumb mixture. Arrange chicken pieces in two 13-x-9-x-2-inch rectangular pans that have been lined with foil. Bake at 350 degrees for 40 minutes. Reverse pans in oven and cook 40 minutes longer. If chicken begins to brown too much cover loosely with foil. Yield: 8 servings.

Note: Orange juice concentrate may be substituted for the pineapple. Chicken may be prepared in advance and refrigerated until desired cooking time.

Mrs. Judy G. Wright
Bel Air Unit (Fallston)

Variation: For sauce: use 1 (20-ounce) can chunk pineapple, 2 tablespoons cornstarch, 3/4 cup vinegar, 1/2 cup sugar, 2 tablespoons soy sauce, 1/2 teaspoon ginger, 1 chicken bouillion cube, 1/2 cup green pepper strips. While chicken is cooking, drain pineapple juice into saucepan. Add water to make 1 1/2 cups. Add remaining ingredients; cook, stirring until thickened. After chicken has baked 30 minutes, remove from oven. Turn pieces over so skin side is up. Pour sauce over all; return to oven and cook 30 minutes more.

Mrs. Walter Harris
Kent County Unit (Chestertown)

CHICKEN PARMESAN

½ cup butter or margarine
1 cup crumbs (cornflake,
   bread or cracker)
⅓ cup Parmesan cheese
1 teaspoon salt

1 teaspoon paprika
¼ teaspoon pepper
2½ or 3 pound broiler-
   fryer, cut up and
   skinned

Melt butter. Mix crumbs, cheese and seasonings in a shallow bowl. Roll chicken in butter and then in the crumb mixture. Place chicken in a baking pan, meat side up, and drizzle any leftover butter over top of chicken. Bake at 325 degrees for 1 hour, basting after ½ hour.

Barbara Comerford Shaeffer
Caroline County Unit (Greensboro)

Lexington Market

129

STUFFED VEAL ROLLS

4 strips bacon
2 cups Stove Top
  seasoned stuffing mix
8 thin veal steaks
1¼ tablespoons bacon
  drippings

1 (10¾-ounce) can cream
  of mushroom soup
⅓ cup milk

In skillet, brown bacon until crisp; save drippings. Prepare stuffing mix according to package directions. Crumble bacon into stuffing. Stir; place ⅓ cup stuffing on each steak. Roll and place toothpicks in each end to hold together. Add bacon drippings to skillet and brown veal. Arrange veal rolls in casserole dish (12-x-8-x-2-inch). Combine soup and milk; heat slightly and pour over veal. Bake in a 350 degree oven for 1 hour. Yield: 8 servings.

Mrs. Thomasina W. Washington
Communities United Unit (Landover)

Maryland's Seafood and Game

The Clam Man—Ruth Westfall

This Maryland waterman is a scene that is native to the Chesapeake Bay area. The income of many of the residents of the Eastern Shore counties is derived from the waters of the Bay from clamming, crabbing, oystering and fishing plus the packaging industry related to the seafood catch.

CRAB RELLENO (STUFFED CRAB)

3 tablespoons oil
1 clove garlic, crushed
2 tablespoons minced
  onion
1 medium tomato,
  chopped
1 cup cubed potatoes
1/4 cup minced celery
1 cup crab meat (cooked
  or canned)

1 teaspoon salt
1/2 cup seedless raisins
  (optional)
1/8 teaspoon pepper
1 teaspoon Accent
6 top shells of crabs
2 eggs, beaten
3/4 cup oil
Bread crumbs
Catsup

In frying pan over medium heat, sauté garlic in oil until golden brown. Add onion and tomato; stir until tomato turns saucy. Add potatoes and stir-fry for 2 minutes; add celery, crab, salt, Accent, pepper and raisins. Stir fry 5 minutes or until potato is cooked. Taste and season if needed. Let cool. Clean crab shells and moisten with a little beaten egg, fill with crabmeat mixture and pack firmly. Dust top with bread crumbs and dip in beaten eggs. Fry, top side down, in 3/4 cup oil until golden brown. Serve hot with catsup. Serves 6.
Note: If crab shells are not available, combine stuffing mixture with 4 beaten eggs and fry as for omelet.

Mrs. David H. Mangle (Pam)
St. Mary's County Unit (Lexington Park)

OUR FAVORITE CRAB CAKE RECIPE

Crumbs from 2 slices
  bread
2 small eggs
3 rounded tablespoons
  mayonnaise
1 teaspoon dry mustard
1 teaspoon salt
1/4 teaspoon pepper

1/2 teaspoon Old Bay
  Seasoning
1/2 teaspoon
  Worcestershire sauce
1 pound lump crab meat,
  picked
Butter or margarine

Blend all ingredients thoroughly except crab. Add crab meat and gently toss to retain lumps. Mold into cakes and fry in butter or margarine until lightly browned. Yield: 8 to 10 cakes.

Gertrude Leamer
Howard County Unit (Ellicott City)

VIP DEVILED CRAB MEAT

3 eggs, hard-cooked
2 tablespoons flour
5 tablespoons butter
2½ cups milk
2 tablespoons chopped
   parsley
1 teaspoon onion, minced
2 cups fresh crab meat,
   picked and flaked

1¼ teaspoons salt
¼ teaspoon Paprika
2 tablespoons Sherry or
   Worcestershire sauce
   (optional)
⅓ cup bread crumbs

Preheat oven to 500 degrees. Separate egg yolks from whites; while still hot, crush yolks with a fork or rice them. Blend with 1½ tablespoons butter. Blend 2 tablespoons flour and 1½ tablespoons butter. Combine yolks and flour mixture. Stir milk in gradually. Cook and stir these ingredients over low heat until they thicken and boil. Add egg whites and remaining ingredients, except crumbs. Pour all into a greased 2-quart casserole. Cover and top with ⅓ cup bread crumbs. Dot with 2 tablespoons butter. Bake in hot oven for about 10 minutes. Watch carefully! Serves 10.

Honorable Marjorie S. Holt
Severna Park Unit (Severna Park)

EASTERN SHORE STEAMED CRABS

12 live Maryland blue
   crabs
2½ tablespoons Old Bay
   Seasoning

3 tablespoons salt
Water or beer
Vinegar

Using a large pot with a cover and a rack 2-inches high, add equal quantities of vinegar and water (or beer) to just below the level of rack. Layer live crabs, sprinkle each layer with seaonings and salt. Cover and steam until crabs are red.
Note: Keep lid on tight as crabs will try to get out of the pot! Recipe can be doubled per dozen.

Rose Mills
Somerset County Unit

SAVORY DEVILED CRAB

1 pound crab meat,
  picked and flaked
2 eggs, hard-cooked and
  sliced
2 tablespoons
  Worcestershire sauce
1/2 cup mayonnaise
1 cup cream
1/2 large onion, chopped
1/2 green pepper, chopped

1 egg, beaten
2 tablespoons India relish
4 tablespoons bacon
  drippings
Salt and pepper to taste
Cornflake crumbs
Butter
Cleaned crab shells or
  ramekins

Mix all ingredients together, except crumbs and butter. Fill crab shells or individual ramekins. Sprinkle top with crumbs and dot with butter. Bake in a 425 degree oven until brown. Serve hot. Serves 6.

Mrs. Charles W. Moore (Jane)
Talbot County Unit (Easton)

CRAB GUMBO

1/4 pound bacon, cut-up
1/4 cup butter
1/4 cup onion, chopped
2 cups okra
1 clove garlic, minced
1/4 lemon, sliced thin
1 (16-ounce) can
  tomatoes
1 bay leaf
3 cups boiling water

1/2 teaspoon salt
1/4 teaspoon paprika
Few drops of Tabasco
  sauce
1 tablespoon
  Worcestershire sauce
2 tablespoons flour
2 cups crab meat, picked
  and flaked

Cook bacon briefly in a heavy kettle; add 2 tablespoons butter and onion and sauté until transparent. Add okra, tomatoes, garlic, lemon and bay leaf. Bring to a boil and add water, salt, paprika, tabasco and Worcestershire. Simmer, partially covered, for one hour. Blend remaining butter with flour and stir into mixture. When thickened, stir in crab, bring to a boil and serve hot. Serves 4 to 6.

Kay G. Bienen, Delegate to House of Delegates
Laurel/Beltsville Unit (Laurel)

ESCALLOPED CRAB

Pick through two pounds of back fin crab. Reserve about 2 tablespoons. Brown 2 cups bread crumbs in ½ cup butter.

Cream sauce:

2 cups half-and-half
2 cups chicken broth
4 slices onion
4 sprigs parsley
8 tablespoons butter
8 tablespoons flour
4 tablespoons freshly
  grated Parmesan
  cheese

Garlic salt
White pepper
Nutmeg
2 tablespoons
  Worcestershire sauce

Scald a mixture of the half-and-half, chicken broth, onion and parsley. Melt butter in a heavy saucepan, stir in butter until smooth, and cook over low heat for several minutes. Do not brown. Strain hot liquid into butter/flour combination and continue cooking over low heat, stirring constantly, until sauce bubbles. Simmer gently for several minutes. Add the Parmesan cheese and stir until melted. Blend in dashes of garlic salt, white pepper, a little nutmeg, and the Worcestershire sauce. Taste and adjust seasonings.

Presentation:

In a buttered oven-proof casserole, spread some of the cream sauce, then some crab, and sprinkle with browned bread crumbs. Season with a little garlic salt and white pepper. Repeat layers to top, ending with cream sauce and bread crumbs. Dot with butter and heat, covered, in a 375 degree oven for 20 minutes. Remove cover and heat for 10 minutes more if needed. Remove from oven; sprinkle top with reserved crab and a little good, red paprika. Serve immediately. Serves 6 to 8.

William Taylor, The Dinner Designer, as presented to Mary Anne Reibsome
St. Mary's County Unit (Great Mills)

CRAB AND MUSHROOM CASSEROLE

½ (10½-ounce) can cream
   of mushroom soup
½ soup can milk
1 egg
¼ cup mayonnaise
¾ cup packaged
   seasoned stuffing
1 (7-ounce) can crab
   meat, flaked

¾ cup sliced fresh
   mushrooms
½ cup diced onion
3 tablespoons margarine
   or butter
½ cup Cheddar cheese,
   shredded

Preheat oven to 350 degrees. Sauté mushrooms and onions in butter until tender. Combine soup and milk with mushroom/onion mixture; beat in egg and mayonnaise. Stir in stuffing mix and gently fold in crab. Pour into a buttered 1½-quart baking dish and top with cheese. Bake for 40 minutes. Serves 4.

Jaye Bauckman
Anne Arundel County Unit (Annapolis)

CRABMEAT SUPREME

1 pound fresh crab meat,
   picked and flaked
2 tablespoons butter
½ cup sherry
2 tablespoons flour
½ teaspoon salt
Dash of pepper

2 cups light cream
2 (10-ounce) packages
   frozen asparagus
1 cup whipped cream
4 tablespoons Parmesan
   cheese

Preheat oven to 400 degrees. Sauté the crab meat lightly in butter. Add sherry and simmer until reduced by half. Add flour, seasonings and cream; cook until thickened. Cook and drain asparagus. Place in a well-buttered casserole and pour crab meat mixture over; spread entire top with whipped cream. Sprinkle with Parmesan cheese and place in oven to brown lightly. Watch it carefully! Serves 4 to 6.

Mrs. Sandi Hollenbeck
Kent County Unit (Chestertown)

CRAB IMPERIAL

1 pound crab meat
2 tablespoons margarine
2 tablespoons flour
3/4 cup milk
1 egg, beaten
1 hard-cooked egg,
chopped fine
1 tablespoon mayonnaise
6 drops Worcestershire
sauce

1/2 teaspoon parsley flakes
1/4 teaspoon seafood
seasoning
1/2 teaspoon dry mustard
1 teaspoon salt
1/4 teaspoon pepper
1 cup bread crumbs
1/4 cup margarine, melted
Cheddar cheese,
shredded (optional)

Preheat oven to 325 degrees. Remove cartilege from crab meat; place in a large bowl. Melt margarine over low heat, add flour and stir to make a paste. Add milk and cook slowly, stirring constantly, until thickened. Reserve 6 tablespoons sauce, add remainder to crab meat, along with raw egg, hard-cooked egg, mayonnaise, Worcestershire sauce, mustard, parsley, and seasonings. Mix gently but thoroughly. Pour into baking shells or a 1 1/2-quart baking dish; top with bread crumbs and melted margarine, then reserved white sauce. Add cheese if desired. Bake for 45 minutes or until brown on top.

Sue Wheeler
Carroll County (Hamstead)
Similar recipes submitted by:
Mrs. George J. Jobson
Kent County (Chestertown)
Note: Mrs. Jobson adds 1 cup finely chopped red and green peppers (mixed) and omits hard-cooked egg.
Gertrude Shockley
Wicomico County Unit (Salisbury)

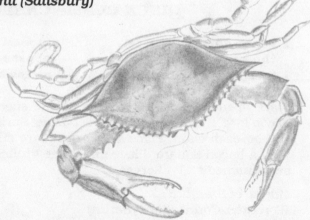

CRAB AND SHRIMP CASSEROLE

1/2 pound shrimp, cooked
1 pound crab meat,
   picked and flaked
1 cup celery, chopped
1 medium onion, chopped
1 cup salad dressing or
   mayonnaise

1 teaspoon
   Worcestershire sauce
Salt and pepper to taste
Bread crumbs for
   topping

Preheat oven to 350 degrees. Combine all ingredients and put into a greased 1½-quart baking dish. Sprinkle bread crumbs on top. Bake for 30 to 40 minutes. Serve hot. Serves 5 to 6.

Mrs. Norman Johnson (Mary Lee)
Harford County--Bel Air Unit (Bel Air)
Variations submitted by:
Mrs. Dorothy Higdon
Montgomery County Unit (Potomac)
Note: Mrs. Higdon substitutes Pepperidge Farm Stuffing Mix for bread crumbs.

Mrs. Pat Harbold
South Charles County Unit (LaPlata)
Note: Mrs. Harbold substitutes 2 cups crushed potato chips for bread crumbs.

Similar recipe by: Mrs. Rebecca Puente
Bel Air Unit

QUICK CLAMS CASINO

2 dozen small clams on
   the half shell
1 teaspoon garlic salt

1/4 pound Provolone
   cheese
6 strips bacon

Place opened clams on a large cookie sheet. Slice cheese and bacon into 1-inch squares and set aside. Sprinkle a dash of garlic salt on each clam. Place a cheese square on each clam and top with a bacon square. Place under the broiler for 5 minutes and serve immediately. Serves 4.

Margaret Bradford
Worcester County Unit (Berlin)

MAYOR HARRY KELLEY'S CLAM CHOWDER

50 clams with juice,
  chopped
1 pound bacon, diced
8 large potatoes, diced
3 medium onions, diced

4 stalks celery, sliced
2 (3-ounce) cans tomato
  puree
Water

Cook clams and bacon in Dutch oven for 30 minutes. Add remaining ingredients and cook for another 40 minutes or until clams are tender.

Harry W. Kelley, Mayor
Ocean City

LOBSTER ALMONDINE

3 cups cooked lobster
3 tablespoons butter
1½ cups Madeirra wine or
  cream sherry
3 cups hot cooked rice

¼ cup almonds
⅓ cup butter, melted
Juice of 1 lemon
Dash of parsley flakes

Sauté lobster in butter for 5 minutes. Add wine; simmer until wine is almost evaporated. Place rice in serving dish. Sprinkle with almonds. Arrange lobster over rice; garnish with butter, lemon juice and parsley flakes. Serves 6.

Mrs. Richard C. Norris
South Potomac Unit (Temple Hills)

OYSTERS GRANDFATHER

Preheat oven to 375 degrees. Scrub oysters to remove sand. Place on rack with drip pan underneath and roast until they pop open. Slide oysters and juice into soup plates which have been coated with fresh, sweet butter, finely chopped parsley, and celery tops. Serve with Maryland beaten biscuits topped with thinly shaved Smithfield ham.

Mary E. Busch
Towson Unit (Baltimore)

OYSTER FRICASSÉE

1 cup butter	3 egg yolks, beaten
1½-quarts shucked oysters	Dash of mace
2 tablespoons flour	Salt and white pepper
1 cup heavy cream	

Melt butter in a heavy skillet. Add oysters and heat for 1 minute. Mix flour with a little cream; stir in remaining cream, egg yolks and seasonings. Cook until thickened, stirring often. Serve at once on toast. May be cooked in a chafing dish. Serves 6.

Marge Seebode
Dorchester County Unit (Cambridge)

FLO'S SCALLOPED OYSTERS

2 cups crushed oyster crackers	½ teaspoon pepper
1 pint oysters, drained	½ cup butter, cut into ¼-inch slices
1 teaspoon salt	2 cups milk

Preheat oven to 350 degrees. Sprinkle one-third of cracker crumbs into a greased 2-quart casserole dish. Spoon half of oysters evenly over crumbs, sprinkle with ½ teaspoon salt and ¼ teaspoon pepper. Place half of butter slices over oysters. Repeat layers. Top with remaining cracker crumbs. Pour milk over oyster mixture. Bake for 45 minutes.

Flo Horney
Queen Annes County Unit (Centreville)

Similar recipes submitted by:

Arnold L. Amass (Skip)
Carroll County Unit (Westminster)

Mrs. Rebecca Simns
Kent County Unit (Rock Hall)

OYSTER BISQUE

½ pound fresh
  mushrooms, sliced
¼ cup butter or margarine
1 cup water
3 egg yolks
2 teaspoons instant
  chicken bouillon
1 cup half and half or
  light cream

¼ teaspoon salt
1 pint fresh oysters,
  undrained
2 to 4 teaspoons dry sherry
6 tablespoons butter or
  margarine

Cook and stir mushrooms in ¼ cup butter until tender. Add water and pour into blender container; cover. Blend on medium speed until mushrooms are coarsely chopped. Gradually blend in egg yolks. Return mixture to saucepan. Stir in chicken bouillon, half and half, and salt. Heat, stirring constantly, until thickened; remove from heat. Using another saucepan, cook oysters over low heat until edges curl. Stir oysters into mushroom mixture. Stir in sherry and heat just until hot. Ladle into bowls; float butter pat in each bowl. Serve with oyster crackers.

Anne R. Jacobs
Dorchester County Unit (Cambridge)

FRIED OYSTERS

1 quart oysters
3 eggs, beaten
½ cup milk
1 box Nabisco cracker
  meal

3 teaspoons salt
3 teaspoons pepper
4 tablespoons oil

Mix eggs, milk, and 1 teaspoon salt and pepper together in large bowl. Sprinkle oysters with remaining salt and pepper. Dip oysters into egg mixture; roll in cracker meal. Using a heavy skillet, fry oysters in hot oil until golden brown. Serves 4.

Frances Jameson
Southern Charles County Unit (LaPlata)

SHRIMP MOLD

1 (8-ounce) package Philadelphia Brand cream cheese
1 (10½-ounce) can tomato soup
2 (4-ounce) cans cocktail shrimp
½ cup onion, chopped
½ cup celery, chopped
1 cup mayonnaise
1 envelope unflavored gelatin
¼ cup cold water

Stir cream cheese and soup together in a pan over low heat until it comes to a boil. Set aside. Dissolve gelatin in water. Add to the soup mixture along with other ingredients; mix well. Pour into a 4 or 5 cup mold and refrigerate until firm. Unmold and serve with party rye bread or assorted crackers.

Julia C. Totten
Southern Charles County Unit (White Plains)

Variations submitted by:
Nancy W. Barrett
Worcester County Unit (Berlin)
Note: May substitute tuna or salmon for shrimp.

Judy Rachap
Annapolis Unit (Annapolis)
Note: Add 3 teaspoons lemon juice to above recipe.

Marion D. Vosseler
Northeastern/Baltimore Unit (Perry Hall)

SPICED SHRIMP

1 cup vinegar
1 tablespoon salt
1 tablespoon paprika
1 tablespoon celery seed
1 tablespoon dry mustard
1 tablespoon red pepper
2 cans beer
4 stalks celery
1 pound raw shrimp, rinsed

Mix above ingredients together in a heavy saucepan (except shrimp) and bring to a boil. Add shrimp to mixture and bring to a boil again; steam for 20 minutes. Serves 4 to 6.

Gordon F. Plett
Merle DuVal Unit (Landover)

SHRIMP JAMBALAYA

1 clove garlic, minced
½ cup onion, chopped
½ cup green pepper,
    chopped
½ cup mushrooms, sliced

4 sliced water chestnuts
1 cup stewed tomatoes
3 cups meat stock or
    bouillon

Sauté garlic, onions, green peppers and mushrooms in oil in a heavy saucepan. Add remaining ingredients and simmer for 45 minutes to 1 hour.

Add:

¾ cup raw rice
¼ teaspoon thyme

¼ cup celery, chopped
1 pound shrimp, shelled

Continue cooking until rice is done and shrimp are red in color. Stir frequently to prevent sticking. Serves 4 to 6.

Note: For 20 people use 4 times the recipe but only 3 pounds shrimp.

Similar recipe contributed by: Mrs. Charles W. Moore (Jane)
Talbot County Unit (Easton)

D. Joan Williams
Dorchester County Unit (Cambridge)

Hooper Island Tongers
David Morehead

SHRIMP DAVIDE

Thick White Sauce:

^{1}/$_2$ cup butter or margarine
^{1}/$_2$ cup flour
1 (13-ounce) can
   evaporated milk or/

1^1/$_2$ cups milk
Salt and pepper

Melt butter in heavy skillet. Stir in flour; add milk slowly, stirring constantly, until thick. Salt and pepper to taste.
Note: Evaporated milk will make a richer sauce!

Casserole:

1 can or frozen package
   artichoke hearts
^{3}/$_4$ pound cooked shrimp
^{1}/$_4$ pound fresh or (4-
   ounce) can drained,
   sliced mushrooms

1^1/$_2$ cups thick white sauce
^{1}/$_4$ cup sherry
1 tablespoon
   Worcestershire sauce
Parmesan cheese,
   grated

Place artichokes in bottom of a 1-quart baking dish. Mix the cream sauce, shrimp, mushrooms, sherry and Worcestershire sauce together. Pour this mixture over the artichokes. Sprinkle with grated Parmesan cheese and bake at 350 degrees until bubbly. Serve over rice. Serves 4 to 6.

Miss Nancy Dick
Kent County Unit (Chestertown)

OPEN-FACED TUNA SANDWICH

1 (6^1/$_2$-ounce) can tuna,
   drained
1 medium onion, chopped
^{1}/$_2$ green pepper, chopped
^{3}/$_4$ cup shredded cheese
   (Cheddar, Swiss or
   combination)

^{1}/$_2$ cup mayonnaise
4 English muffins, split
   and lightly toasted

Combine first 5 ingredients. Spread about ^{1}/$_4$ cup of mixture on each muffin half. Put on cookie sheet and broil for about 3 minutes. Cheese will be melted; onion and green pepper will still be crisp. Yield: 3 to 4 servings.

Emily Guard
Laurel/Beltsville Unit (Laurel)

SHRIMP-CRABMEAT CASSEROLE

2 cups onion, chopped
2 cups celery, chopped
2 medium green peppers, chopped
1/4 cup butter or margarine, melted
2 cups cooked wild rice
2 cups cooked white rice
2 pounds shrimp, peeled, deveined and cooked
2 (6-ounce) packages frozen crabmeat, thawed

3 (10³/₄-ounce) cans cream of mushroom soup
1/2 cup water
2 (4-ounce) cans sliced mushrooms, drained
1/2 cup slivered almonds
1 (2-ounce) jar sliced pimento, drained
1 cup breadcrumbs, divided

Preheat oven to 350 degrees. Sauté onion, celery, and green pepper in butter until tender but not brown. Add remaining ingredients except bread crumbs. Stir well. Spoon mixture into two lightly greased 2-quart baking dishes; sprinkle each with 1/2 cup bread crumbs. Bake for 1 hour or until bubbly. Serves 15 to 20.

Ellen Myers
Queen Annes County Unit (Queenstown)

BLUEFISH IN BEER BATTER

1 large bluefish (3 to 5 pounds)
1 1/2 cups flour
3 tablespoons baking powder

2 teaspoons salt
1 teapoon lemon-pepper
3 eggs, beaten
10 ounces beer

Sift flour, baking powder, salt and pepper together. Add the eggs and beer to flour mixture. Skin whole fish and remove the dark streak from the sides of fish; fillet and cut into serving size pieces. Place the fillets in the batter and let set for about 20 minutes. Remove and deep fry at 350 degrees until golden brown.
Note: Extra batter can be used to fry oysters - without the fish odor! I've used this recipe dozens of times and get raves about it each time!

Mrs. Ruth R. Wilt
Western Charles County Unit (Indian Head)

IMPERIAL BLUEFISH

1 pound Bluefish fillets   **Mayonnaise**

Lay Bluefish fillets on a rack in a broiling pan. Coat top with mayonnaise. Place about 6 inches away from broiler and broil until the mayonnaise is golden brown and the fish flakes with a fork. Remove and let fish cool enough to handle. Once cooled, discard the mayonnaise and any of the dark brown areas of meat, leaving only white meat. Shred white meat.

Casserole:
Fish
Dry bread crumbs from
   2 slices white bread,
   crusts removed
¹/₂ cup mayonnaise
1 tablespoon Dijon
   mustard
1 tablespoon
   Worcestershire sauce

1 tablespoon fresh
   lemon juice
1 tablespoon chopped
   parsley
¹/₄ teaspoon Old Bay
   Seasoning
Dash hot pepper sauce

Mix fish with remaining ingredients. Pour into a buttered 1¹/₂-quart baking dish. Bake in a preheated 350 degree oven for 30 minutes or until it bubbles slightly. Serves 4.
Note: What does one do with all that beautiful Bluefish from the Chesapeake Bay? It makes a tasty substitute for crab meat!

Carole A. Glowacki (Mrs. Gerald)
Towson Unit (Glen Arm)

STUFFED FLOUNDER

1 medium onion, finely
   chopped
2 stalks celery, finely
   chopped
¹/₄ cup butter or margarine
1 egg
1¹/₂ cups milk
3 tablespoons sour cream
3 tablespoons lemon juice
2 tablespoons
   mayonnaise

3 cups soft bread crumbs
1 pound fresh or canned
   crab meat
1 tablespoon parsley
1 teaspoon salt
1 teaspoon cayenne
4 flounders, dressed
   (1¹/₂ to 2 pounds)
¹/₂ cup water

Preheat oven to 375 degrees. Sauté onions and celery in ¼ cup butter; stir until tender. Beat eggs in a bowl and add milk, sour cream, mayonnaise and lemon juice and bread crumbs. Stir in onions and celery. Add crab and parsley, salt and pepper. Cut fish along back bone; carefully split from center to outside edges to make a pocket. Stuff pocket with crab meat and fasten with skewers. Bake for 45 minutes, basting fish with ½ cup butter three or four times. Serves 4.

Dorothy Hettche
Queen Annes County Unit (Queenstown)

ROCK FISH BAKE

4 pounds rock fish
1 teaspoon salt
¼ teaspoon pepper
1 (4-ounce) can
mushroom pieces

6 tablespoons butter
2 tablespoons flour
Milk
⅓ cup dry white wine

Preheat oven to 350 degrees. Drain mushrooms; reserve liquid. Sauté mushrooms in 3 tablespoons butter and set aside. Melt 3 tablespoons butter in skillet, add flour and stir. Add milk combined with mushroom liquid to make 1½ cups. Cook over medium heat, stirring constantly for 1 minute. Remove from heat and gradually stir in wine. Add mushroom pieces. Rub fish with salt and pepper. Place in a greased baking dish, pour sauce over fish, and bake for 1 hour. Baste fish several times with pan juices while baking. Pour extra sauce over rock to serve. Garnish with lemon wedges.
Note: May be complimented with crab meat or wild rice stuffing. Add more seasoning to taste.

Dorothy Bailey
Queen Anne Unit (Centreville)

BAKED FISH WITH EGGPLANT

Eggplant-Tomato Sauce:

1 (16-ounce) can
   tomatoes,
   cut-up
³/₄ cup tomato juice
   cocktail
1 eggplant, pared and
   diced
¹/₂ cup onion, chopped
¹/₄ cup celery, diced
¹/₄ cup dry white wine
1 small banana pepper,
   seeded and chopped

2 tablespoons parsley
2 tablespoons olive or
   salad oil
1 tablespoon
   Worcestershire sauce
2 teaspoons sugar
1 teaspoon basil
¹/₄ teaspoon thyme
¹/₄ teaspoon oregano

In a saucepan, combine all ingredients. Bring to a boil; reduce heat and cook gently, uncovered, until thickened. (About 40 minutes.) Stir ocassionally while cooking. Use as directed below.

Casserole:

2 pounds fresh or frozen
   fish fillets, thawed
Olive or salad oil
Salt, pepper and
   paprika
3 cups fresh mushrooms,
   sliced

1 (14-ounce) can
   artichoke hearts,
   drained and halved
1 recipe eggplant-tomato
   sauce

Preheat oven to 400 degrees. Place fish in a greased 13-x-9-x-2-inch baking dish. Brush with a little oil; sprinkle with salt, pepper and paprika. Bake, uncovered, for 15 minutes. Add mushrooms and artichokes; spoon eggplant-tomato sauce over all. Cover; return to oven and bake for 20 minutes more. Serve with hot cooked rice. Serves 8.

Mrs. Tom Fairfax (Darlene)
Western Charles County Unit (Marbury)

SWEET AND SOUR FISH

Beer batter:
1 cup beer
2 cups flour
1 egg

¼ teaspoon salt
2 pounds fish fillets

Combine all ingredients, except fish. Allow to rest for 4 hours. Cut fish fillets into bite-sized pieces. Dip into beer batter and deep fry. Place in oven to keep warm.

Vegetables:
Green peppers
Mushrooms
Onions
Snow peas
Carrots

Celery
Bamboo shoots
Water chestnuts
Pineapple chunks

Cook any combination of the vegetables in a very hot skillet in oil just until tender crisp. Be sure to include green peppers and pineapple chunks. Use ½ to 1 cup of each vegetable.

Sauce:
1 cup pineapple juice
½ cup distilled white vinegar
½ cup firmly packed brown sugar

2 tablespoons oil
2 tablespoons soy sauce
¼ teaspoon pepper
3 tablespoons cornstarch

Combine above ingredients. Bring to a boil, stirring constantly, and cook for 2 minutes. Combine fish and vegetables on a platter. Pour sauce over and mix just to coat. Serve over hot rice. Serves 4 to 6.

Wanda L. Jackson
Cecil County Unit (Elkton)

CANADIAN GOOSE

½ cup dry red wine
⅔ cup Campbell's beef
   broth
½ teaspoon tarragon
½ teaspoon thyme

1 Canadian goose
1 medium onion
1 stalk celery
Salt

Combine the first 4 ingredients. Marinate the goose for 2 or 3 hours in this mixture. Quarter the onion and cut celery stalk into 3 or 4 pieces and put both into cavity of goose. (This takes away the wild flavor.) Sprinkle goose with salt and place into a roaster, breast side down, with the marinade. Cover and bake at 325 degrees for 2 hours or until tender. Baste several times. Roast breast side up, uncovered, for the last 15 minutes.

NOTE: LEFTOVER GOOSE

1 can Campbell's beef
   broth
¼ cup red wine
1 tablespoon cornstarch
¼ cup water
2 cups diced, cooked
   goose

2 (3-ounce) cans sliced
   mushrooms
1 box long grain and
   wild rice mix

Heat broth and wine in saucepan. Mix cornstarch and water to make a paste; add to broth and stir until thickened. Add goose and mushrooms, heat through. Serve over rice. Makes 3 or 4 servings.

Lois Nagle
Bel Air Unit (Bel Air)

WHAT'S UP DOC RABBIT CASSEROLE

1 package herbed instant
  rice
½ cup butter or
  margarine, cut-up
8 half chicken breasts or
  rabbit meat, filleted
1 (10½-ounce) can cream
  of chicken soup

1 (10½-ounce) can cream
  of celery soup
1 (10½-ounce) can cream
  of mushroom soup
½ soup can sherry
½ pound Cheddar cheese,
  shredded
Chopped almonds

Preheat oven to 275 degrees. Place rice in a 12-x-8-x-2-inch baking dish; add butter, chicken or rabbit. Pour over 3 cans soup mixed with sherry. Cover with cheese and sprinkle on almonds. Bake, uncovered, in a slow oven 2½ to 3 hours. Serves 4 to 6. *Note: Good dish for entertaining when dinner may be delayed since it can be kept hot for additional time.*

Dr. Donald B. Rae
Dorchester County Unit (Cambridge)

CURRIED PHEASANT CASSEROLE

1 pheasant
Salt
2 slices onion
6 whole allspice
1 stalk celery
1 (10½-ounce) can cream
  of celery soup
¼ cup pheasant broth

1 (4-ounce) can
  mushrooms, drained
½ teaspoon parsley flakes
¼ teaspoon curry powder
2 tablespoons chopped
  pimentos
Paprika

Preheat oven to 350 degrees. Cut pheasant into serving pieces; cover with salted water. Add onion, allspice and celery. Bring to a boil and simmer until tender. When cool, slice and cube meat. Combine soup, pheasant broth, mushrooms, parsley, curry powder and pimentos. Add pheasant and mix lightly. Place in a buttered 2-quart casserole. Sprinkle with paprika and bake, covered, for 40 to 45 minutes. Serve over hot rice, potatoes, or buttered toast. Serves 4.

Amy Crisp
North Central Unit (Randallstown)

FRED'S FRICASSEED MUSKRAT

3 muskrats
½ cup flour
2 tablespoons shortening
½ teaspoon salt
Dash of pepper

2 onions, sliced and/or
½ pound bacon, sliced small
2 pints water

Cut muskrats into serving pieces. Soak in salted water for 5 hours changing water several times. Drain and dredge in flour. Brown in hot shortening in a heavy skillet. Salt and pepper as you fry. Remove pieces and pour off excess fat. Place muskrats back into pan; add onions and/or bacon and water. Cover and bake at 350 degrees for 1 hour.

Variation: For sour muskrat, add 1 pint vinegar and 1 pint water in place of 2 pints water.

Senator and Mrs. Frederick C. Malkus, Jr.
Dorchester County Unit (Cambridge)

Salad, Soups and Dressings

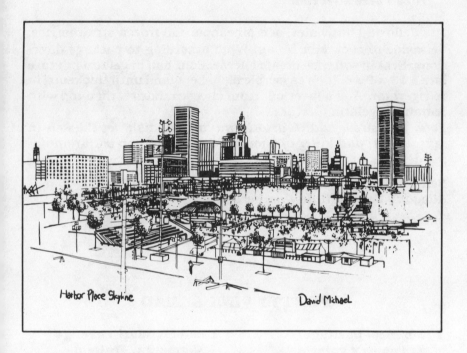

Harbor Place Skyline — David Michael

Harbor Place—David Michael

Harbor Place is a recently developed attraction designed to beautify Baltimore Harbor and the city of Baltimore.

STRAWBERRY JELLO SALAD

2 (3-ounce) packages
strawberry Jello
2 cups boiling water
1 (9-ounce) can crushed
pineapple, drained
1 (16-ounce) box sliced
frozen strawberries

1 (3-ounce) package
Philadelphia Brand
cream cheese
1 envelope Dream Whip
Milk

Mix Jello and hot water; add pineapple and frozen strawberries. Set aside to cool. Mix Dream Whip according to package directions. Beat in softened cream cheese. Pour half of gelatin mixture into a 13-x-9-x-2-inch casserole dish. Let stand until thickened in refrigerator. Add a layer of cream cheese mixture, then top with remaining gelatin mixture.
Note: If desired, add ⅔ gelatin mixture to dish, let thicken in refrigerator; add layer of cheese mixture and top with remaining gelatin; swirl with a knife; refrigerate to set.

Bonnie Martin
Allegany County Unit (Cumberland)

PRETTY PINK SALAD

1 (3-ounce) package
strawberry gelatin
1 cup boiling water
1 (3-ounce) package
cream cheese
1 (9-ounce) can crushed
pineapple

1 can Mandarin orange
segments, drained
1 cup miniature
marshmallows

Combine gelatin with ¾ cup hot water. Stir until dissolved. Add softened cream cheese to remaining ¼ cup hot water and stir until soft. Mix with gelatin. Drain pineapple; measure juice and add enough water to juice to make 1 cup liquid. Add liquid, pineapple, and orange segments to gelatin mixture. Stir in marshmallows. Pour into mold and chill until firm. Serves 10.

Sandra W. Younger
Calvert County Unit (St. Leonard)

CHRISTMAS SALAD

First Layer:

1 (3-ounce) package
  raspberry gelatin
1 cup boiling water
1 cup whole cranberry
  sauce

½ cup pecan pieces
  (optional)

Dissolve gelatin in boiling water until clear. Add cranberry sauce; chill until mixture is consistency of egg whites. Add nuts. Pour into an 8-x-8-x-2-inch pan or large mold. Chill until firm.

Second Layer:

1 (3-ounce) package
  lemon gelatin
1 cup boiling water
1 (3-ounce) package
  cream cheese

1 cup crushed pineapple,
  partially drained
½ cup miniature
  marshmallows

Dissolve gelatin in boiling water until clear. Add cream cheese to hot gelatin mixture and beat until smooth. Add pineapple and marshmallows; let set until it begins to thicken; pour over first layer and chill until firm.

Third Layer:

1 (3-ounce) package lime
  gelatin
1 cup boiling water

1 (1 pound) can fruit
  cocktail

Dissolve gelatin in boiling water. Add ½ cup syrup drained from fruit cocktail. Add drained fruit cocktail. Pour over first two layers. Chill until firm. Unmold. Decorate as you see fit. Serves 10 to 12.

Ruth Michel
Western Charles County Unit (Indian Head)

WALNUT CRANBERRY DELIGHT

2 (3-ounce) packages
raspberry or strawberry
gelatin
2 cups cranberry juice
cocktail, heated
2 cups bitter lemon
carbonated beverage

1 cup walnuts, chopped
1 cup raw cranberries,
chopped
1 (11-ounce) can
Mandarin oranges,
drained

Dissolve gelatin in hot cranberry juice. Stir in lemon beverage
and refrigerate until partially set. Fold in remaining ingredients
and pour into a greased 1½ quart ring mold. Chill until firm.
Serves 8 to 10.

Joanne Olszewski
First District Harford Unit (Joppa)

SALAD OF GOLD

1 (3-ounce) package
lemon gelatin
²/₃ cup boiling water
²/₃ cup syrup, drained
from pineapple
2 tablespoons vinegar

²/₃ cup evaporated milk
2 (3-ounce) packages
cream cheese
1 cup carrots, cut into
pieces
²/₃ cup pineapple, drained

Place gelatin and hot water into a blender container, cover and
process at stir until dissolved. Add syrup, vinegar, and milk.
Push liquify. Add cream cheese. Push blend. Add carrot pieces
and pineapple. Blend again. Pour mixture into a 2-quart ring
mold. Chill until set. Serves 8.

Sherry Noren
Caroline County Unit (Denton)

PATIO SALAD

1½ cups pineapple juice
1 teaspoon curry powder
1⅓ cups Minute Rice
1½ cups chicken, cooked
and cut into bite-sized
pieces
½ cup celery, diced

½ cup dill pickle, chopped
1 teaspoon onion, grated
1 (10-ounce) package
frozen green peas
Dash of pepper
¾ cup mayonnaise or
salad dressing

Add curry powder to pineapple juice and bring to a boil. Add rice, cover, and remove from heat. Let stand 5 minutes; fluff rice with a fork. Add chicken, celery, pickles, onion, peas and pepper. Mix well and chill. Before serving toss with mayonnaise, using a fork. Serve on salad greens garnished with tomatoes. Serves 4 to 6.

Nancy Wegstein
Montgomery County Unit (Gaithersburg)

PINK ARTIC FREEZE

2 (3-ounce) packages
  cream cheese
2 tablespoons
  mayonnaise
2 tablespoons sugar
2 cups (1 pound can)
  whole cranberry sauce

1 cup (9-ounce can)
  crushed pineapple,
  drained
1/2 cup walnuts, chopped
1 (8-ounce) container
  Cool Whip

In large mixing bowl, soften cream cheese; blend in mayonnaise and sugar. Add fruit and nuts; fold in Cool Whip. Pour into an 8½-x-4½-x-2½ inch loaf pan or a large ring mold. Freeze until firm or overnight. To serve, let stand at room temperature for 15 minutes, slice, and place on a bed of lettuce. Serves 8 to 10.

Penny Seymore
Northwest Community Unit (Randallstown)

WINTER BEAUTY SALAD

1 cup hot water
1/3 cup red cinnamon
  candies
1 package lemon gelatin
1½ cups applesauce

2 (3-ounce) packages
  cream cheese
1/2 cup nuts, chopped
1/2 cup celery, chopped
1/2 cup mayonnaise

Pour hot water over cinnamon candies and gelatin. Stir until dissolved. Add applesauce. Pour half of the mixture into an 8-inch square pan; chill until firm. Blend cream cheese, nuts, celery, and mayonnaise together. Spread on top of the gelatin mixture. Pour on remaining half of gelatin and refrigerate until set. Serves 6 to 8.

Phyllis Teets
Garrett County Unit

CABBAGE SOUFFLÉ

1 (3-ounce) package
lemon gelatin
1 1/2 cups hot water
2 tablespoons vinegar
1/2 cup mayonnaise
Salt and pepper
2 cups cabbage, shredded

1 tablespoon onion,
chopped
2 tablespoons green
pepper or pimento,
chopped
Dash celery seed

Dissolve gelatin in hot water. Add vinegar, mayonnaise, and seasonings. Let set until it begins to thicken; beat until fluffy. Fold in remaining ingredients. Pour into mold or loaf pan. Refrigerate until set. Serves 6 to 8.

Rebecca Welsh
Caroline County Unit (Denton)

OVERNIGHT SALAD

1 medium head of lettuce,
torn into bite-sized
pieces
2 medium red onions,
peeled and sliced
1 (16-ounce) can LeSeur
peas, drained

6 slices bacon, fried and
crumbled
1 cup mayonnaise
1/2 cup Parmesan cheese

Layer the lettuce in a 10-x-14-x-2 inch Tupperware container, followed by a layer of peas, then onions, then bacon. Spread mayonnaise over all, being sure to cover well. Sprinkle with Parmesan cheese. Seal tightly with lid and refrigerate overnight. Cut into squares before serving. Serves 6 to 8.

Kathryn B. Wisegarver
Washington County Unit (Hagerstown)

SAUERKRAUT SALAD

1 (16-ounce) can
  sauerkraut
1/2 cup sugar
1 cup celery, diced
1 cup green pepper,
  diced
1/4 cup onion, diced

1/4 teaspoon salt
Dash pepper
1 teaspoon celery seed
3 tablespoons diced
  pimento
3 tablespoons vinegar

Drain sauerkraut for about 15 minutes; cut fine with kitchen shears. Add remaining ingredients and stir to mix. Cover and store in the refrigerator for 24 hours. Serves 6 to 8.

Edythe Jolley
Dorchester County Unit (Cambridge)

CONROY'S CAESAR SALAD

1 clove garlic, peeled
1/8 teaspoon salt
1/8 teaspoon pepper
1 teaspoon dry mustard
3 tablespoons lemon juice
3 tablespoons Italian
  olive oil
Dash Worcestershire
  sauce

1 coddled egg
2 bunches romaine
  lettuce
1 tablespoon Parmesan
  cheese, grated
1/2 cup croutons

Rub garlic, salt, and pepper into a wooden salad bowl. Add dry mustard and lemon juice and stir thoroughly. Add olive oil, stir thoroughly. Add Worcestershire sauce, stir thoroughly. Add coddled egg and stir until mixture is quite creamy and frothy. Wash and dry romaine lettuce, tear into bite sized pieces and add to salad bowl. Sprinkle with parmesan cheese and toss gently. Toss once again with croutons and serve. Yields 6 servings.

Senator Edward T. Conroy
Bowie/GlenDale/Kettering/Largo Unit (Bowie)

FRUITED CHEESE SALAD

2 pounds cottage cheese
1 quart frozen whipped
  dessert topping
2 (3-ounce) packages
  orange-pineapple
  gelatin

1 (13½-ounce) can
  pineapple tidbits,
  drained
1 (11-ounce) can
  Mandarin orange
  segments, drained

Using a mixer, blend cottage cheese and topping until thoroughly mixed. Stir in *dry* gelatin; fold in fruit. Press into a 7-or 8 cup mold. Chill overnight. Serves 12.

Betty A. Armacost
Carroll County Unit (Westminster)

FRENCH DRESSING

½ cup oil
1 tablespoon lemon juice
⅓ cup granulated sugar
1 teaspoon salt

¼ cup cider vinegar
½ cup catsup
1 teaspoon paprika
Onion salt to taste

Mix above ingredients in a wide mouth jar; cover and shake vigorously. Refrigerate and use on tossed green salad or grapefruit-and-avocado salad.

JoAnne Bayles
Montgomery County Unit (Rockville)

BLUE CHEESE DRESSING

¼ teaspoon garlic powder
1 teaspoon celery salt
½ teaspoon paprika
½ teaspoon black pepper
2 tablespoons wine
  vinegar

1 pint sour cream
½ cup mayonnaise
½ pound blue cheese,
  crumbled

Mix all ingredients, except cheese, until well blended. Carefully fold in blue cheese. Refrigerate overnight before using.

Ruth Bernard
Towson Unit (Towson)

FRENCH ONION SOUP

2 tablespoons butter or
  margarine
2 tablespoons vegetable
  oil
6 to 7 cups (2 pounds)
  thinly sliced yellow
  onions
1/2 teaspoon sugar
2 tablespoons flour
5 cans (10 1/2 ounce)
  condensed beef broth
  (bouillon)

4 soup cans water
1 teaspoon salt
Dash freshly ground
  pepper
Cheese-garlic flavored
  croutons
2 cups shredded
  mozzarella cheese

In a 4-to-6 quart Dutch oven or kettle heat butter and oil until hot. Add onions and sugar, cooking slowly for even browning. Stir frequently until onions are lightly browned and bottom of pan is lightly glazed, approximately 20 to 30 minutes. Scrape glaze from bottom of pan and blend in with onions. Stir in flour and cook 1 minute. Stir in beef broth, water, salt and pepper. Bring to a boil. Reduce heat and simmer, covered, for 30 minutes. Preheat oven to 450 degrees. Pour soup into a large ovenproof soup tureen or individual earthenware soup bowls. Place croutons on surface of soup and sprinkle with cheese. Bake in 450 degree oven for 10 to 15 minutes or until cheese is melted and bubbling. Serves 10.

Maureen Trenary
North Charles County Unit (Waldorf)

PEANUT BUTTER SOUP

1 teaspoon minced onion
2 tablespoons butter
5 tablespoons peanut
  butter
2 tablespoons flour

2 cups canned chicken
  broth
1 cup milk
Salt and pepper
1/2 cup heavy cream

Brown onions in butter. Stir in peanut butter. Gradually add flour; stir in chicken broth and milk. Season to taste with salt and pepper. Simmer about 30 minutes; stirring until smooth. Add heavy cream before serving. Serves 4.

Grace E. Hanley
Montgomery County Unit

TURKEY NOODLE SOUP

1 cup turkey, chopped
5 cups turkey broth
¾ cup celery, chopped
1 large carrot, grated
2 chicken bouillon cubes
¼ cup onion, chopped

Salt
Pepper
2 tablespoons parsley
 flakes
3 cups wide egg noodles

Using a four-quart saucepan, combine all ingredients except noodles. Salt and pepper to taste. Bring to a boil and add noodles. Cook one-half hour or until noodles are tender. Serve hot.
Note: This is a good way to use holiday turkey leftovers. Pieces of skin and fat from turkey can be used for flavor during cooking if removed before serving.

Margaret Brinsfield
Dorchester County Unit (Vienna)

CHICKEN SOUP

3 chicken breasts, split
 or 1 stewing hen
 (liver removed)
6 cups water
1 medium onion, diced
4 carrots, diced
4 stalks celery, sliced

1 tablespoon dry or 3
 sprigs parsley
8 medium to large
 mushrooms
2 cups thin egg noodles
 or alphabets
5 chicken bouillon cubes

Place chicken in a 4-quart Dutch oven. Pour in water (may fill to within 1 inch of top of pot). Add onion, carrots, celery, parsley, mushrooms; bring to a boil and simmer for 1½ to 2 hours, or until chicken is fork tender. Remove chicken to plate. Dissolve bouillon in broth and add noodles. Cook until tender (about 10 to 15 minutes. Remove chicken from bones, dice). Return chicken to broth. Remove from heat and allow to cool. Skim fat from soup when completely cool. Serves 8 (1-cup servings).

Susie Woods (Mrs. Lou)
Glen Burnie Unit (Glen Burnie)

GREEN LIMA BEAN SOUP WITH DUMPLINGS

1 piece salt pork or ham bone
1 (No. 10) can whole tomatoes
6 cups water
3 cups green lima beans
1 cup corn, yellow or white
3 small potatoes, cubed
1 tablespoon sugar
½ teaspoon Worcestershire sauce
Salt
Pepper

Combine ham bone, tomatoes, and water in large Dutch oven or saucepan. Cover and simmer about one hour. Add remaining ingredients. Adjust seasonings to taste. Simmer while preparing dumplings (about 45 minutes). Add dumplings and cook at a rolling boil for 20 minutes.

DUMPLINGS

2 cups flour
1 teaspoon salt
2 teaspoons baking powder
2 teaspoons oil
Water to moisten

Mix above ingredients well. Add enough water to make a stiff dough. Roll thin on floured board and cut into two-inch squares.

George P. Mahoney
Northern Baltimore County Unit (Ownings Mills)

Teackle Mansion

Built 1801

SOUTHERN MARYLAND OYSTER STEW

4 tablespoons butter or
  margarine
1 medium onion, chopped
  fine
3 large potatoes, cubed in
  1/2 inch squares
1/2 cup water

1 teaspoon salt
1 quart milk
1/2 teaspoon celery salt
Dash of pepper
1 pint raw oysters, with
  liquor
Paprika

In large frying pan or 3 quart saucepan, melt butter or margarine over medium heat. Add chopped onion and cook until soft. Add water, potatoes, and salt; cover and cook until potatoes are done. Add milk, celery salt, and dash of pepper. Stir and heat to nearly boiling over medium heat. Add oysters and continue heating until edges of oysters curl, stirring ocassionally to prevent burning. Sprinkle with paprika. Serve piping hot with crisp crackers or buttered toast. Serves 8.

Margaret J. Johnson
Western Unit (Marbury)

Variation:

submitted by H. Hurtt Deringer for Quarter Neck Landing Oyster Stew:
Add 1/2 cup each of green pepper, chopped, fresh mushrooms, and celery, chopped, when onion is added in above recipe.

H. Hurtt Deringer
Kent County Unit (Chestertown)

V-8 VEGETABLE SOUP

1 pound beef, ground or
  cubed
1 (46-ounce) can V-8
  vegetable juice
1 cup rutabaga, chopped
  and pre-cooked
2 cups celery, chopped

2 onions, chopped
3 potatoes, chopped
1 (20-ounce) can mixed
  vegetables
2 cups cabbage, chopped
Salt and pepper to taste

Using a 6 to 8 quart soup pot, combine beef, V-8 juice, rutabaga, celery, onions, and potatoes. Cook until vegetables are almost done. Add mixed vegetables and cabbage and cook until tender. Add water as necessary to keep vegetables covered. Serves 6 to 8.

Martha Gebo
Worcester County Unit (Pocomoke)

EASY VEGETABLE SOUP

1 pound chuck beef,
cubed
3 tablespoons oil
2 cups water
1 large onion, chopped
1 large bag frozen mixed
vegetables

1 (16-ounce) can
tomatoes
Pinch thyme
Pinch basil
1 large green pepper,
chopped
1/2 cup chopped celery

Sauté beef cubes in oil; add water and onion. Simmer for 1 hour. Add mixed vegetables, tomatoes, thyme and basil; bring to a boil and simmer about 30 minutes. Add green pepper and celery and simmer for about 1 hour longer.

Leonora Jones
Rosemont/Edmondson Unit (Baltimore)

OYSTER STEW

2 tablespoons all-purpose
flour
2 tablespoons cold water
1 1/2 teaspoons salt
1 teaspoon
Worcestershire sauce

Dash bottled hot pepper
sauce
1 pint shucked oysters,
undrained
1/4 cup butter
4 cups milk, scalded

In saucepan blend flour, water, salt, Worcestershire sauce, and hot pepper sauce. Stir in undrained oysters and butter. Simmer over very low heat, stirring gently, until edges of oysters curl, 3 to 4 minutes. Add hot milk; remove from heat and cover. Let stand 15 minutes. Reheat briefly. Float pats of butter and oyster crackers atop, if desired. Serves 4 to 6.

Mary Jane Frere
Charles County Unit (Bel Alton)

MOM MOM STEVENS' CRAB SOUP

1 quart tomatoes
1/2 pound bacon, diced
1/2 head medium cabbage,
  chopped
8 potatoes, diced
4 onions, diced
4 stalks celery, diced
4 carrots, sliced
1 turnip, diced
1 quart lima beans,
  fresh or frozen

1 quart green beans,
  fresh or frozen
2 cups cut corn, fresh
  or frozen
1 pound lump crab meat
1 pound claw crab meat
Salt and pepper to taste
Dash red pepper
Old Bay Seasoning, if
  desired

Cook bacon and tomatoes for one-half hour in large saucepan or Dutch oven. Add cabbage and cook until tender to the fork. Add potatoes, onions, celery, turnip and carrots and cook until tender. Add beans and corn and cook one-half hour. Season to taste. When all vegetables have cooked until flavors blend, add crab meat and mix thoroughly.

Note: A tablespoon of sugar helps to bring out the flavor and cuts the acid of the tomatoes. One large bag of frozen mixed vegetables may be substituted for the beans and corn. Flavor of this soup is best the second day. Soup freezes well for a short time, but there is seldom any left over! If freezing, add pepper lightly as the flavor tends to get strong with freezing.

Nila Kay Coleman
Kent Unit (Chestertown)

CLARK'S FAVORITE CRABMEAT SOUP

4 (10½-ounce) cans
  tomato soup
4 (10½-ounce) cans pea
  soup
6 soup cans milk
1 pint heavy cream
  (slightly beaten)

2 pounds fresh lump crab
  meat
½ teaspoon salt
Dash pepper
½ cup sherry (optional)

Heat all ingredients in a large saucepan, except the sherry, just to the boiling point. Remove from heat. Add sherry if desired. Serve hot.

J. Clark Barrett
Towson Unit (Baltimore)

Tender Extras

Chesapeake Bay Puppies—Beebee Winterbottom
Chesapeake Bay Retrievers and Black Labrador Puppies—Water dogs and retrievers of the Chesapeake Bay area.

HOMEMADE DOG FOOD

4 cups or 2 pounds
ground scrap meat
1½ cups grated carrots
1½ cups cooked green
beans

1 cup beef or chicken
bouillon
1 cup cooked rice or ¾
cup cottage cheese
(small curd)

Mix all ingredients in a large saucepan. Simmer for about 10 minutes. Package in serving-sized containers and freeze, if desired.

Note: This is a good way to incorporate vitamin supplement in food. If older dog has a weight problem, use cottage cheese instead of rice. For spoiled dog you can serve on Lennox china and garnish with parsley.

Oliver T. Brinsfield
Dorchester County Unit (Vienna)

BAKED HOMINY GRITS WITH CHEESE

1 cup quick hominy grits
4 cups boiling water
1 teaspoon salt
Dash of Tabasco
1 cup milk

1 cup medium sharp
Cheddar cheese,
shredded
3 tablespoons butter
2 eggs, well beaten

Add grits to boiling salted water, cover; cook over low heat for 15 minutes. It will be a good mushy texture. Let cool a little. Add salt, Tabasco and milk and stir well. Add cheese; mix; then add butter, beating after each tablespoon. Add eggs and beat until smooth. Season to taste with salt and pepper. Pour into well buttered baking dish. Sprinkle with a little finely shredded cheese. (Optional) Bake in preheated 375 degree oven for 45 minutes, until puffy and golden brown. Serve immediately. Serves 6.

Louise C. Dennison
Caroline County Unit (Goldsboro)

Similar recipe submitted by:
Jack Glover
Wicomico County Unit

ONE-DISH BRUNCH

10 slices Canadian bacon
8 (1-ounce) slices Swiss
 cheese
8 eggs
Salt and pepper to taste
1 cup light cream

2 tablespoons Parmesan
 cheese
1 can sliced pineapple
1/2 cup raspberry jam
2 tablespoons melted
 butter

Arrange bacon around edge of deep-dish pie pan to form scalloped edge. Line bottom with Swiss cheese slices. Break raw eggs carefully over cheese; add salt, pepper, cream and Parmesan cheese. Bake for 15 to 20 minutes at 350 degrees. Remove from oven. Drain pineapple slices, place on cookie sheet, brush with jam, drizzle on melted butter; broil for 7 to 8 minutes. Place pineapple slices on top of eggs and serve in the dish the eggs were baked in.

Shirley Dugan
St. Mary's County Unit (Hollywood)

Variation: For Brunch Puff: 12 slices of white bread, quartered, 8 slices bacon, 3 medium onions, 1/2 pound Swiss cheese, 8 eggs, 4 cups milk, 1 1/2 teaspoons salt and pepper. Place half of bread in a greased 13-x-9-x-2-inch pan. Sprinkle with half of the bacon and sliced onions, which have been cooked, and cheese. Repeat layers. Combine eggs, milk, salt and pepper. Pour over layers and refrigerate overnight. Bake at 350 degrees for 45 to 50 minutes. Serves 8.

Gwen Braden
Aberdeen/Havre de Grace Unit (Churchville)

Variation: For Breakfast Casserole use: 1 pound sausage, browned, drained and cooled; 6 eggs, well beaten; 2 cups milk; 6 slices bread, crust removed and cubed; 1 teaspoon salt; 1 teaspoon dry mustard; 1 cup cubed Cheddar cheese. Beat the eggs well and add all the other ingredients. Put in 9 by 9 inch square dish or 13-x-9-x-2-inch rectangular dish. Place in refrigerator several hours or overnight. Bake 45 minutes at 350 degrees.

Mary A. Shimoda
Glen Burnie Unit (Glen Burnie)

Mary Lee Webster
Dorchester County Unit (Cambridge)

EASTER GELATIN EGGS

1 (3-ounce) package
lemon-flavored gelatin
1 (3-ounce) package lime-
flavored gelatin
1 (3-ounce) package
strawberry-flavored
gelatin

2 cups hot water, divided
1 cup pineapple juice
1 cup orange juice
1 cup ginger ale
21 egg shells

Dissolve lemon-flavored gelatin in ²/₃ cup hot water. Add 1 cup orange juice. Dissolve lime-flavored gelatin in ²/₃ cup hot water; add 1 cup ginger ale. Dissolve strawberry-flavored gelatin in ²/₃ cup hot water; add 1 cup pineapple juice. Make a small hole in the end of an egg shell. Shake the egg out. Rinse shell with cold water and drain and dry. Fill egg shells with one of the gelatin mixtures. (Each gelatin mixture will fill 7 egg shells.) Refrigerate upright in egg carton. Crack shells and remove gelatin eggs. Serve on deviled egg dish on green tinted coconut. Can also use lime jello put through a potato ricer and it looks like grass.

Augustabelle W. Miller
Calvert County Unit (St. Leonard)

SPINACH OMELET

1 (10-ounce) package
spinach, prewashed
2 tablespoons olive oil
¼ cup fresh creamery
butter
1 medium onion, minced
1 small garlic clove,
mashed

Pinch of salt
Pinch of freshly ground
black pepper
2 slices Italian salami
or prosciutto, diced
4 eggs, beaten
3 tablespoons grated
Parmesan cheese

Wash the spinach and drain well. Place olive oil and butter in a skillet and heat. Add onion and garlic and cook slowly until light brown. Add spinach, stir, cover and cook for 15 minutes. Add salt, pepper and salami or prosciutto and cook for 2 minutes. Pour eggs into spinach and stir. Cook until done to taste. Sprinkle cheese on top. Serves 3.

Alma Lauriente
Howard County Unit (Clarksville)

GRANOLA

6 cups old fashioned oats
3 cups unsweetened
  shredded coconut
1 cup wheat germ
1 cup sunflower seed
1 cup sesame seed
1 cup honey

½ cup corn or safflower
  oil
1 cup cold water
1 cup slivered blanched
  almonds
1 cup raisins and/or
  chopped dates

Preheat oven to 225 degrees. In a large mixing bowl combine oats, coconut, wheat germ, sunflower seed, and sesame seed. Toss to mix. Add honey and oil, stirring until well-mixed. Add cold water a little at a time, stirring until mixture is crumbly. Pour into a heavy baking pan that has been lightly brushed with oil. Spread mixture evenly. Place on middle rack of oven; bake for 2 hours, stirring every 15 minutes. Add almonds, raisins and/or dates. Cool.

Note: Mixture should be lightly browned and should feel crisp to the touch when done. Cereal should be stored in a cool dry place or it may be frozen for future use. All ingredients can be purchased in health food stores.

Rheta Brenza
Glen Burnie Unit (Glen Burnie)

CORN FRITTERS

1½ cups flour
2½ teaspoons baking
  powder
1 teaspoon salt

1 (20-ounce) can cream-
  style corn
1 egg, slightly beaten

Sift dry ingredients, combine corn and egg. Stir corn and egg mixture into sifted dry ingredients until just blended. Drop batter by tablespoons into hot fat. Fry about 4 minutes, turning once during frying. Cook until golden brown. Yield: 10 to 12 fritters.

Note: Serve with maple syrup, butter or jelly. Also very good with ham or poultry.

Sandra J. Cain
Northern Charles County Unit (Waldorf)

Variation submitted by
Mrs. Freida Farrell
Communities United Unit

171

APPLE PANCAKE TIER

Pancakes:
6 eggs
1 cup all-purpose flour
1 teaspoon salt
½ teaspoon nutmeg

1 cup milk
¼ cup butter or
    margarine, melted

Beat eggs thoroughly in a large mixing bowl; beat in flour, salt, and nutmeg on low speed until moistened. Stir in milk and melted butter or margarine. Pour 1 cup batter into each of 3 greased 9-inch pie or cake pans. Bake at 400 degrees until pancakes are light brown and puffy (they will curl at edges). This will take 15 to 20 minutes. Prepare apples while pancakes bake.

Apples:
6 cooking apples, peeled,
    cored and sliced
¼ cup butter or
    margarine, melted

½ cup sugar
2 teaspoons grated lemon
    peel, fresh or dried

Cook and stir apples in ¼ cup butter in frying pan for 5 minutes. Stir in sugar. Cook until apples are tender, about 10 minutes. Place 1 pancake on serving plate, top with ⅓ of apple mixture, ⅓ of lemon peel. Repeat process with remaining pancakes, apples and lemon peel. Sprinkle powdered sugar over tiers and serve with warm syrup for dinner or brunch. Yield: 6 to 8 servings.

Tom Fairfax
Western Charles County Unit (Marbury)

OLD FASHIONED EGG NOODLES

1 beaten egg
2 tablespoons milk

1 to 1¼ cups all-purpose
flour

In mixing bowl, combine egg, milk and ½ teaspoon salt. Add enough flour to make a stiff dough. Roll dough thinly on floured surface. Let stand 20 minutes. Roll up loosely and slice ¼-inch wide. Unroll, cut noodles; spread out. Let dry for 2 hours. Use in chicken soup or any soup.

Mrs. Helen Carter
Annapolis Unit (Annapolis)

Vegetables

'The Dome' Johns Hopkins Hospital

"The Dome" of John Hopkins Hospital—David A. Dulik

This hospital and university has been the hub of much cancer research in recent years. John Hopkins Hospital and its dome have been a Baltimore landmark since 1889. Hopkins' major cancer research efforts began in 1977. Its Onoclogy Center houses highly advanced patient care facilities, a dozen basic research programs and over 50 full-time scientists seeking the causes and cures of many forms of cancer.

BARLEY AND MUSHROOMS

1/2 cup margarine or
   butter
2 medium onions,
   chopped
1/4 pound mushrooms,
   sliced

1 cup medium pearl
   barley
3 cups chicken broth

Preheat oven to 350 degrees. Sauté onions and mushrooms in margarine; add barley and 2 cups of chicken broth. Pour into buttered 1 1/2-quart baking dish and bake for 1 hour, covered. Add more broth as needed during baking. Add remaining broth and bake about 1 hour more.

Susan H. Whitaker
South County Unit (Arnold)

WANDA'S GREEN BEANS

3 tablespoons oil
1 cup onions, sliced
1 (8-ounce) can
   mushrooms
2 (16-ounce) cans green
   beans, drained

1 cube chicken or
   vegetable bouillon
1 teaspoon thyme
1/4 teaspoon pepper
2 tablespoons soy sauce

Heat oil over medium-high heat. Add onions and sauté until soft. Add mushrooms and sauté for 1 minute, stirring often. Add green beans and stir rapidly for 1 minute. Add remaining ingredients and stir to coat beans. Reduce heat to low and cover. Cook for 3 minutes more. Serve hot. Serves 4.

Wanda Young
Communities United Unit

BROCCOLI BAKE

2 (10-ounce) boxes frozen
   chopped broccoli
1 (10 1/2-ounce) can cream
   of mushroom soup
1 egg, slightly beaten

Salt and pepper to taste
1/2 cup mayonnaise
1/2 cup butter, melted
1 cup croutons or bread
   crumbs

Preheat oven to 350 degrees. Cook broccoli as directed and drain well. Add soup, egg, mayonnaise, salt and pepper to broccoli and pour into a 2-quart casserole which has been buttered. Toss butter and croutons together and sprinkle over broccoli. Bake for 45 minutes.

Mrs. W. A. Leeson (Loraine)
Lanham/Bowie Unit (Lanham)

Variations submitted by the following:
Jane Driver (Howard County Unit) suggests adding 1 cup chopped onion and 1 cup crushed cheese crackers to replace croutons.

Nancy Barr (Garrett County) suggests adding ¹/₂ cup cheese to casserole.

Col. Dorothea L. Rancourt (USA-RET.), Montgomery County Unit adds 1 teaspoon Worcestershire sauce to recipe.

Susan Whitaker (South County Unit,) suggests adding 1 can sliced water chestnuts and substituting celery soup for the mushroom soup.

Mrs. Bonnie Blunt (Caroline County Unit) adds 1 can French-fried onions to the top of the casserole.

SWEET AND SOUR RED CABBAGE

¹/₂ cup butter	1 teaspoon allspice
2 tablespoons instant onions	¹/₄ teaspoon cloves
¹/₄ cup brown sugar	1 (2-pound) red cabbage, finely shredded
1 teaspoon salt	¹/₂ cup boiling water
¹/₂ teaspoon pepper	¹/₂ cup wine vinegar

Melt butter in skillet; sauté onions until golden brown. Add sugar, seasonings and shredded cabbage. Mix lightly. Add water, cover and simmer for 1 hour. Add wine vinegar and simmer, covered, for 10 minutes longer. Yield: 4 to 6 servings.
Note: This is pleasantly tart; should you prefer it milder, use only ¹/₄ cup vinegar.

Vivian Lewis
Communities United Unit

BAKED CARROTS

2 cups carrots, cooked
and mashed
³/₄ cup sugar
3 eggs, beaten
¹/₂ cup butter, melted

¹/₂ teaspoon salt
3 tablespoons flour
2 teaspoons baking
powder

Preheat oven to 400 degrees. Mix all ingredients together and pour into a greased 9-x-5-x-3-inch casserole. Bake for 15 minutes; reduce heat to 350 degrees and continue cooking for 45 minutes. Serves 4 to 6.

D. Norma Plaikey
Howard County Unit (Columbia)

CORN PUDDING (PENNSYLVANIA DUTCH STYLE)

1 (16-ounce) can corn,
drained
2 eggs, slightly beaten
2 tablespoons flour

2 tablespoons sugar
1 cup milk
Salt and pepper to taste
¹/₂ cup butter

Preheat oven to 300 degrees. Mix all ingredients together. Pour into a 2-quart buttered casserole dish. Bake in a slow oven for one hour.

Madelyn M. Hollis
Queen Annes County Unit (Centreville)

Similar recipes submitted by:

Betty Stone
Queen Annes County Unit
Betty Roney
Washington County Unit

BAKED CORN

1 tablespoon flour
1 to 2 tablespoons sugar
¹/₂ teaspoon salt
1 cup milk

2 eggs, well-beaten
2 cups corn, fresh,
frozen, or canned
1 tablespoon butter

Preheat oven to 325 degrees. Mix dry ingredients together; stir in milk, eggs and corn. Pour mixture into a well buttered 9-x-5-x-3-inch casserole dish and dot with butter. Place in oven and bake about 50 to 60 minutes or until a knife inserted in the center comes out clean. Yield: 4 servings.

Betty Roney
Washington County Unit (Hagerstown)

EGGPLANT SCALLOPINI

1 tablespoon olive oil
2 tablespoons butter
1 cup chopped onion
3 cloves garlic, crushed
1/2 teaspoon salt
1 whole bay leaf
4 cups peeled and cubed eggplant
1/2 teaspoon salt
1 pound mushrooms, chopped

1/4 teaspoon pepper
1 cup chopped green peppers
2 medium-sized tomatoes, chopped
1/4 cup tomato paste
1 cup Marsala or dry white wine
1/4 cup chopped parsley
1 cup Parmesan cheese
Pasta

Over medium temperature, heat olive oil and butter in a large, heavy skillet. Add onions and garlic, salt and bay leaf. Sauté for 5 minutes. Add the eggplant and another 1/2 teaspoon salt. Cook, covered, 10 minutes, stirring occasionally. Add mushrooms, basil, peppers, tomatoes and tomato paste. Mix well and simmer, covered 10 minutes. Add wine and parsley and simmer, covered over low heat for about 15 to 20 minutes. Just before serving, mix in the grated Parmesan cheese. Serve over pasta, and pass extra Parmesan cheese. Yield: 4 to 6 servings.
Note: This takes approximately one hour to prepare. During the last 10 minutes of simmering time, prepare pasta and a salad. Highly nutritious vegetarian meal!

Caroline Davis-Robinson
St. Marys County Unit (Lexington Park)

ESCALLOPED EGGPLANT

1 medium eggplant, sliced
  crosswise ¹/₂-inch thick
1 or 2 medium tomatoes,
  sliced
1 large onion, thinly
  sliced
³/₄ cup butter or
  margarine, melted

¹/₂ teaspoon salt
¹/₂ teaspoon basil
¹/₄ pound mozzarella
  cheese, sliced
¹/₂ cup packaged dried
  bread crumbs
2 tablespoons grated
  Parmesean cheese

Preheat oven to 450 degrees. On medium-sized heat-proof platter, arrange eggplant slices, then tomato and onion slices. Drizzle with melted butter. Sprinkle with salt and basil. Bake, covered for 20 minutes. Cut mozzarella slices into thirds; arrange over top. Stir crumbs into remaining butter; sprinkle over top, then top with Parmesan cheese. Bake, uncovered, for 10 minutes or until cheese is bubbly. Yield: 4 servings.

Gertrude D. Reid
Kent County Unit (Chestertown)

MUSHROOM BUSINESS

6 slices buttered bread,
  cubed
¹/₂ cup mayonnaise
1 pound fresh
  mushrooms, sliced
  and sautéed
¹/₂ cup green peppers,
  chopped
¹/₂ cup onion, chopped

¹/₂ cup celery, chopped
  and sauteed
1¹/₂ cups milk
2 eggs, beaten
Salt and pepper to taste
1 (10¹/₂-ounce) can cream
  of mushroom soup
¹/₂ cup Parmesan cheese

In a buttered 2-quart casserole, place 3 slices of bread, cubed. Add mayonnaise to mushrooms, peppers, onions and celery. Mix well and spread over bread in casserole. Pour remaining bread on top of casserole. Refrigerate for 5 hours or overnight. Before baking add mushroom soup. Bake at 325 degrees for 50 minutes. During last 10 minutes of baking, sprinkle cheese on top. Yield: 4 to 6 servings.

Jean Masonis
Greater Laurel/Beltsville Unit (Laurel)

OLD STYLE SCALLOPED POTATOES

6 medium potatoes, sliced thin
2 onions, sliced thin
3 stalks celery, sliced thin
2 tablespoons chopped green parsley
2 tablespoons flour
1 teaspoon salt
1/2 teaspoon pepper
7 tablespoons butter
2 1/4 cups hot milk

Preheat oven to 325 degrees. Layer one-third of potatoes, onions, and celery into a buttered 2-quart casserole dish. Sprinkle with some of parsley, flour, salt and pepper; dot with butter. Repeat layers until all ingredients are used. Pour hot milk over all. Cover and bake for 1 hour or until potatoes are tender. Add more milk if mixture becomes dry. Yield: 4 servings.

Debbie Scott
Queen Annes County Unit (Church Hill)

PEAS AU GRATIN

2 (10-ounce) packages
frozen green peas,
cooked and drained
1 (5-ounce) can sliced
water chestnuts,
drained

1 (10½-ounce) can cream
of mushroom soup
1½ cups sharp Cheddar
cheese, shredded

Preheat oven to 350 degrees. Combine peas and chestnuts with soup and cheese. Pour into a lightly greased 2-quart casserole dish. Bake for 25 to 30 minutes. Serves 6 to 8.

Mary Burgess
South County Unit (Davidsonville)

EASY RICE CASSEROLE

½ cup butter or margarine
1 (10½-ounce) can
chicken broth
1 (10½-ounce) can onion
soup

1 (4-ounce) can
mushrooms, stems and
pieces, undrained
1½ cups raw rice

Preheat oven to 350 degrees. Melt butter in a 1½-quart casserole. Stir in chicken broth and onion soup, mushrooms and rice. Bake for 1 hour. Yield: 6 servings.

Mrs. Norbert DiGiacomo (Jane)
Aberdeen/Havre de Grace Unit (Maryland)

EASTERN SHORE BAKED TOMATOES

1 (16-ounce) can
tomatoes
1 cup sugar
Pinch of salt
¾ teaspoon cinnamon
½ teaspoon nutmeg

Cloves (optional)
3 slices bread or biscuit,
crumbled
4 tablespoons flour
3 tablespoons butter

Preheat oven to 400 degrees. Pour tomatoes into bowl; add sugar, bread and seasonings. Mix well. Pour into a buttered 9-x-5-x-3-inch loaf pan. Sprinkle top with a little more sugar. Bake for 20 to 30 minutes. Let cool before cutting into squares.

Mary Jenkins
Dorchester County Unit (Cambridge)

SWEET POTATO CASSEROLE WITH TOPPING

3 cups cooked sweet potatoes	2 eggs
	1 teaspoon vanilla
1 cup sugar	1/2 cup milk

Preheat oven to 350 degrees. Combine above ingredients in a bowl. Pour into a greased 2-quart casserole dish.

Topping:

1/3 cup butter	1 cup walnuts or pecans,
1 cup brown sugar	chopped
1/2 cup flour	

Mix topping in a bowl; sprinkle over sweet potatoes. Bake for 30 to 35 minutes, uncovered. Serves 4 to 6.

Cheryl L. Willey
Dorchester County Unit (Cambridge)

SUMMER SQUASH CASSEROLE

2 pounds summer squash (can mix yellow and zucchini)	1 cup sour cream
	1/2 cup onions, chopped
	2 medium carrots,
1/2 cup margarine, melted	chopped
1 bag Pepperidge Farm Seasoned Stuffing mix	2 tablespoons chopped pimiento
1 (10 1/2-ounce) can cream of chicken soup	

Preheat oven to 350 degrees. Slice and cook squash until tender but firm. Drain well. Melt margarine and mix with stuffing. Pat 1/2 of stuffing into the bottom of a 13-x-9-x-2-inch baking dish. Add chicken soup, sour cream, onions, carrots, and pimento to squash; pour over crumbs. Add remaining crumbs to top of squash. Bake for 45 minutes. May be frozen and reheated. Enjoy!

Joan Williams
Dorchester County Unit (Cambridge)

Similar recipes submitted by the following:

Helen Stetson
Montgomery County Unit (Silver Spring)

Evelyn T. Tippett
Caroline County Unit (Ridgely)

ZUCCHINI CASSEROLE WITH TOMATOES

1 clove garlic
1 cup onion, sliced
$1/2$ cup green pepper,
   sliced
2 tablespoons salad oil
3 cups zucchini, sliced
   $1/2$-inch thick
1 ($14^{1/2}$-ounce) can
   tomatoes, or

3 fresh tomatoes, sliced
1 teaspoon salt
$1/4$ teaspoon pepper
$1/2$ cup Parmesan cheese
$1/4$ cup shredded Cheddar
   cheese

Preheat oven to 350 degrees. Sauté garlic, onion and peppers in oil. Add zucchini and cook for 2 minutes. Pour into a 13-x-9-x-2-inch casserole dish and add tomatoes, salt and pepper. Bake for 20 to 25 minutes or until zucchini is tender. Sprinkle with cheese and bake a few more minutes until it is melted.

Charlotte Hiner
Worcester County Unit (Berlin)

TOMATO BREAD PUDDING

2 quarts fresh tomatoes,
   peeled and chopped
2 cups crumbled biscuit
$2/3$ to 1 cup sugar,
   depending on sweetness
   of tomatoes

$1/4$ teaspoon ground
   nutmeg

Preheat oven to 325 degrees. Mix all ingredients together lightly and pour into a greased 13-x-9-x-2-inch casserole. Bake for 45 minutes. Dish is done when firm and browned around the edges. Serves 6 to 8.
Note: This recipe will be successful only if homemade biscuits are used! It is four generations old. I feel certain it was designed for use during the great Maryland tomato season!

Mrs. E.O. Clarke, Jr. (Penny)
North Central Unit (Baltimore)

Index

Winter in Ocean City—Gaines Reynolds Clore

Ocean City is a year-round resort. Ocean City's beach is a beautiful place to stroll, breathing in the fresh salt breeze. Winter time weekends find many a vacationer enjoying peace and quiet from a cozy vantage point, and spring brings the best of everything as Ocean City freshens up for another summer season. For conventions, happy reunions or quiet companionship . . . there's a lot to like in Ocean City . . . all year round.

INDEX

MARYLAND'S FLAVOR

American Cancer Society, Maryland Division, Inc.
200 East Joppa Road
Towson, Maryland 21204

Please send _____copies of Maryland's Flavor at $6.00 per copy plus $1.25 per copy for postage and handling.

I enclose an additional donation of $_____

Enclosed is my check or money order for $_____

Name _____

Address _____

City _____County _____State _____Zip __

Enclosed you will find names and addresses for gift cookbooks. I understand you will enclose a gift card with my name for each gift cookbook.

MARYLAND'S FLAVOR

American Cancer Society, Maryland Division, Inc.
200 East Joppa Road
Towson, Maryland 21204

Please send _____copies of Maryland's Flavor at $6.00 per copy plus $1.25 per copy for postage and handling.

I enclose an additional donation of $_____

Enclosed is my check or money order for $_____

Name _____

Address _____

City _____County _____State _____Zip __

Enclosed you will find names and addresses for gift cookbooks. I understand you will enclose a gift card with my name for each gift cookbook.

Re-OrderAdditionalCopies